W9-ANR-809

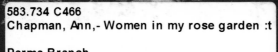

JACKSON
DISTRICT
LIBRARY
A PLACE TO DISCOVER

In memory of:

Irene Gilmore

Donated by:

Parma Countryside

Club

Women in my Rose Garden

Women in my Rose Garden

THE HISTORY, ROMANCE AND ADVENTURE OF OLD ROSES

Ann Chapman

With photographs by Paul Starosta

PALAZZO

This edition published in Great Britain in 2014 by

Palazzo Editions Ltd
2 Wood Street
Bath
BA1 2JQ
www.palazzoeditions.com

Publisher: Colin Webb
Art Director: Bernard Higton
Managing Editor: Judy Barratt
Consultant Editor: Caroline Harris
Copy Editor: Charlotte de Grey
Editorial Assistant: Stephanie Bramwell-Lawes
Picture Researcher: Sophie Hartley

A CIP catalogue record for this book is available
from the British Library.

The moral rights of the author have been asserted.

ISBN: 9780957148338

Printed and bound in China by Imago.

Contents

Introduction 6

Cornelia Africana 10

Félicité and Perpétue Jacques 14

Rosamund de Clifford 20

Jeanne de Montfort 24

Yolande d'Aragon 28

Jeanne d'Arc 32

Marie, Comtesse de Blois 38

Amy Robsart 42

Mary Stuart, Queen of Scots 48

Nur Mahal 54

Margaret, Duchess of Portland 60

Maria Teresa, Princesse de
Lamballe 64

Empress Joséphine 70

Aimée Dubucq de Rivéry 76

Marie de Sombreuil 82

Adélaïde d'Orléans 86

Marie Thérèse, Duchesse
d'Angoulême 90

Louise Antoinette,
Duchesse de Montebello 96

Duchesse d'Auerstädt:
Louise Aimée Julie Leclerc
and Jeanne Alice de Voize 102

Zoé, Comtesse du Cayla 106

Marie Louise, Grand Duchess
of Parma 112

Grace Darling 116

Anaïs Ségalas 122

Queen Victoria 126

Gertrude Jekyll 132

Marie-Henriette, Duchesse
de Brabant 136

Lady Alice Hillingdon 140

Ellen Willmott 144

Julie, Baroness Rothschild 148

Edith Cavell 152

Helen Wilson 156

Constance Spry 160

Nancy Steen 164

Ghislaine de Féligonde 170

Picture Credits 174

Acknowledgements 175

Introduction

"I am not an armchair gardener. For the last forty years of my life I have broken my back, my fingernails and sometimes my heart in the practical pursuit of my favourite occupation."

Vita Sackville-West, *Even More for Your Garden*, 1958

In our garden in New Zealand, I am surrounded by women: Mme de Sombreuil and Ghislaine de Féligonde, Queen Victoria and Grace Darling, Nur Mahal and Mary Queen of Scots. Finding and growing old roses is still my obsession, and in the garden we developed at Trinity Farm we nurtured one-and-a-half thousand plants.

Over twenty-five years ago, I arrived with my family to ten acres of bare land. We were refugees from the rigours of serious jobs in Wellington, drawn to the tranquillity of the countryside around Otaki. We set about developing a three-acre garden based on our twelve years' experience of living in England, with its wonderful gardens of charm and grandeur.

We were not prepared for the vigour our climate gave to the roses, or for our increasing mania for collecting these treasures. But our garden was big enough to allow the roses to grow as they wanted: unrestrained, uninhibited and glorious. Developing a garden also provided some respite from a new career in local government; I was able to put aside the angst of politics and give myself instead to digging, planning and planting.

Trinity Farm has more than one-hundred-and-twenty-five roses named after women. Some are old roses, others more modern, and their inspirational namesakes span the centuries from the age of the ancient classics, through French, German and English history, to newcomers in our own times.

As I worked among these evocatively named roses, I came to wonder about the women who had inspired them. Who were they, and why had they been honoured with a rose? During the celebrations for the centenary of women's suffrage in New Zealand, I started more serious research to find out. It has taken many years to blossom.

Not only do the roses I have chosen for this book grace my own garden – and would be worthy of a place in any – but the women after whom they are named have fascinating, important and world-changing stories to tell.

The rose 'Ellen Willmott'.

Why did rose breeders select a particular woman to honour with a rose? In some cases, it is easy to understand the connection. In others there seems to be no personal relationship; perhaps, we may be permitted to assume, rose growers are romantics at heart, and some women, and the stories of their lives, struck a note that they responded to.

Many hundreds of rose varieties have been named after real women, along with the mythical figures and literary heroines. Some were noted for their courage, others are aristocrats or empresses, collectors or garden designers, each with a rich history of their own. They were daring or provocative in their own right, and did not need their husbands or fathers to make their mark in history. Others are the wives or daughters of nurserymen, or women who purchased the rights to create a rose in their name.

Brent Dickerson explains in *The Old Rose Adventurer*: "The Dutch and the Flemings, who grew the first roses, sent them to us with names which were emphatic and often ridiculous. Soon flower growers called to their aid mythology and history both ancient and modern. Sovereigns, ministers, magistrates, men of war, illustrious men of all nations, celebrated women – all gave their names to many varieties of roses. Now that the number of varieties increases each year by hundreds, nurserymen and fanciers go to the route of dedicating their newcomers to kin and friends." His book often gave me my first clue to unearthing the stories of the women in my own garden.

My references have been wide and varied. I have sourced information from history, biography and rose books. For reasons of space, not all of my seven hundred or so references have made it to the bibliography. I acknowledge all my sources, and I apologise if your contribution has not been listed.

In the writing of this book, there have been moments of laughter and despair, of confrontation with the differing views of different people, and of dealing with the tyranny of the web with all its frustrations, while appreciating the rich knowledge caught within it.

My thanks to my family, Lloyd, Laurence and Nicole, for their supportive bullying and help with research, and to Jocelen Janon for his translations from his native French, and assistance in solving the many

mysteries (to the English speaker) of the French written word. Joanne Knight, as past president of The Heritage Rose New Zealand, has been invaluable in her assistance, freely passing on her knowledge and wisdom. The librarians in the Kapiti libraries have excelled themselves in coping with my sometimes obscure demands. Last, but not least, my thanks to Libby, who continued working in the garden while I was writing this. We have now sold Trinity Farm and, under a new guardian, rose heritage continues to flourish.

Essentially, this book hopes to create an interest in the history of old roses, stirred, not by the evolution of breeding or by botanical intellect, but by the historical romance that is integral to them. Their legacy is more than old breeders or botanical evolution. Their survival is wrapped in the arms of the women who carry their names into history in more ways than cold, historical, intellectual arrogance.

It is a different kind of history that comes alive in our gardens, somewhat removed from the drudgery of classrooms, and this book is for all of you with thanks.

Ann Chapman

Cornelia with her sons, in a detail from *The Mother of the Gracchi* (c.1780) by Joseph Benoit Suvée (1743–1807).

Cornelia Africana

*c.*190–100 BC

C ornelia was one of the most remarkable women in Roman history. She was idolised as the matriarch of the reforming Gracchi family in the time of the Roman Republic, and written about by Cicero and Plutarch. In a society in which women could not formally participate in politics, Cornelia was sought after for her advice, intelligence and political acumen. She inspired her husband and sons, and her family was revered – but also suffered tragically – for its role in improving the quality of life of the poorest Romans.

The mother of the Gracchi became a legendary figure in Roman literature, so that it can be difficult to disentangle the real, historical Cornelia from the myths that surround her.

Daughter of Cornelius Scipio Africanus, who had defeated Hannibal during the Second Punic War, Cornelia married the noble, well-connected and considerably older consul Tiberius Sempronius Gracchus in her late teens. Under her husband's rule, the province of Hither Spain – a region of Hispania roughly occupying the north-eastern coast and the Ebro Valley of modern-day Spain – became one of the most peaceful in the Roman dominions. They had twelve children, but only three survived to reach adulthood: a daughter, Sempronia, and two sons, Tiberius and Gaius. It was the two sons who were to become champions of the people.

Cornelia was admired particularly for her virtue and fidelity, as well as her sharp intellect, and she won the confidence of many important Romans of the period. She was devoted to her children, and is said to have declared them to be her most precious jewels. Cornelia appears to have had a profound influence on them throughout their lives. Their father died while they were still young, and the children were diligently educated by their mother. The philosopher and politician Cicero wrote that Cornelia's sons were nourished more by her conversation than by her breast.

Groomed by Cornelia, Tiberius and his younger brother Gaius became political activists. Travelling through Tuscany on his way to a military campaign, Tiberius noted the deplorable condition of Italian agriculture. Land had passed into the hands of a wealthy elite and was being worked by slaves. When he was elected tribune of the plebs (the ordinary landowning public) in 133BC, Tiberius set about agrarian reform. He redistributed the large holdings into smaller ones, to be farmed by the common people.

Inevitably these measures, and the way that Tiberius had forced them through, brought him into conflict with the Roman Senate and the wealthy classes. The Senate's opposition became so great that it declared his election invalid. Riots followed, and Tiberius and many of his followers were assassinated on Rome's Capitol hill.

Ten years later, Gaius took up his brother's mantle and leadership of the populist movement, proposing a programme of even wider-ranging reforms. When elected tribune (in 123BC and again in 122BC), he gave the lower classes more constitutional powers, as well as instituting more land reforms. Cornelia is said to have pleaded with him not to use the same methods as his murdered brother, but to no avail.

Fragments of letters, thought to be from Cornelia to Gaius, are rare surviving examples of the writings of Roman women of the time, although not all historians accept them as being by Cornelia. Appearing in documents by the first Latin biographer, Cornelius Nepos, one extract reads: "May Jupiter not for a single instant allow you to continue in these actions nor permit such madness to come into your mind. And if you persist, I fear that, by your own fault, you may incur such trouble for your entire life that at no time would you be able to make yourself happy."

Gaius's reforms were viewed as revolutionary by the Senate, and history repeated itself when he met the same inevitable opposition. According to some versions of the events, Gaius killed himself with his slave's sword; some thousands of his supporters were slain alongside him.

After the deaths of her beloved sons, Cornelia continued to work the political system of Rome as much as she could. The historian Plutarch wrote: "Cornelia is reported to have borne all her misfortunes in a noble and magnanimous spirit, and to have said of the sacred places where her sons had been slain that they were tombs worthy of the dead which occupied them."

The democratic movement begun by the Gracchi family, and Cornelia's influence, continued to grow, and eventually became the chief instrument in controlling the power of the few in ancient Rome.

The rose 'Cornelia'

Type of rose: Hybrid Musk
Introduced: 1925
Breeder: Pemberton, Essex, England
Parentage: Unknown

'Cornelia' is one of the prettiest and more enduring of Pemberton's Hybrid Musk roses. Her flowers are a mixture of apricot pink and yellows, with small blooms hanging in arching sprays and a soft, rich, musky fragrance. The blooms develop in luscious clusters, with tight buds opening flat to paler hues.

This rose can climb but is happy as a tall shrub, carrying lots of handsome, small, dark, leathery foliage, which first appears with a bronzy tone. The wood is an interesting claret colour and contrasts nicely with the blooms, which appear continuously throughout the season, well into autumn, when 'Cornelia' is perhaps at her very best. She adapts well to shade and, like her classical sisters, she is healthy in our garden and she appears immune to disease in our climate.

The Reverend Joseph Pemberton (1852–1926), who bred this rose, was vicar of Romford in Essex, and dabbled in rose growing in his spare time. After retirement, he founded a nursery with his sister Florence, and created a new family of roses: the Hybrid Musks. With their strong perfume and repeat flowering, they fitted the new mood among rose growers. He clearly had a love of mythology and many of his roses are named after classical women. Pemberton believed in minimal pruning and, if you follow the little-and-often method, 'Cornelia' will reward you lovingly with a splendid shape and many flowers, and her pervasive perfume will enchant any who pass by her. She will do splendidly as a hedge, climb on a pillar, and grow as a shrub surrounded by a rich mixture of perennials. The legacy both of Cornelia and of her sons, as well as of the Reverend Pemberton, is much cherished in our garden.

Félicité and Perpétue Jacques

Felicitas and Perpetua
died 203AD

The rose 'Félicité-Perpétue' is unusual in that it is named for two girls: the twins Félicité and Perpétue Jacques, daughters of rose breeder Antoine Jacques, who named his girls after the saints Felicitas and Perpetua. Jacques was gardener at the Château de Neuilly, which belonged to the Duc d'Orléans, Louis-Philippe, the "Citizen King" of France from 1830 to 1848. The twins were born in 1827, on 7 March, the feast day of their namesakes – but apart from this little is known about them.

According to the story of the rose, Jacques had reserved one seedling from his latest crop at Louis-Philippe's estate near Paris to be named in honour of his expected baby. Up until this time, and then afterwards, his roses honoured the Duc's family – but this one rose was to be his exception.

However, Jacques faced a dilemma when his wife delivered not one child, but twin girls. So he decided to name that single rose after both his daughters. The Orléans family had a particular attachment to Carthage and had endowed a chapel there – and no doubt this association, together with the Saints' Day on which Jacques's daughters were born, had brought these particular saints and their story to his attention.

Félicité and Perpétue may not themselves have led exceptional lives, but, some two thousand years before, the two Christian saints after whom they were named suffered a terrifying martyrdom in Roman-controlled Carthage, in modern-day Tunisia. During the Roman Emperor Septimius Severus's persecution of the Christians, Felicitas and Perpetua were thrown to wild beasts in the amphitheatre at Carthage because they refused to worship the Roman gods. Their experiences and visions are described in "The Passion of Saints Perpetua and Felicitas", a text that scholars believe to be a genuine historical account and that, it is claimed, was written by Perpetua and one of her fellow accused, Saturus, while in prison, with witnesses later adding an account of their deaths. If Perpetua, aged about twenty-two and the mother of an unweaned child, truly composed this text, it is the earliest text written by a Christian woman.

Vibia Perpetua and her slave Felicitas, who was eight months pregnant, were seized and imprisoned with another slave and two free men, and later Saturus. "The Passion" describes Perpetua's arguments with her father,

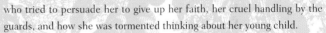

who tried to persuade her to give up her faith, her cruel handling by the guards, and how she was tormented thinking about her young child.

"Then Tertius and Pomponius, the blessed deacons who ministered to us, obtained with money that for a few hours we should be taken forth to a better part of the prison and be refreshed. Then all of them going out from the dungeon took their pleasure; I suckled my child that was now faint with hunger," says the moving account. Perpetua was then allowed to keep the child with her, raising her spirits so that: "Suddenly the prison was made a palace for me ... I would sooner be there than anywhere else." Perpetua had visions in prison of a bronze ladder leading to heaven, with swords to either side: "I went up, and I saw a very great space of garden, and in the midst a man sitting, white-headed, in shepherd's clothing, tall, milking his sheep; and standing around in white were many thousands."

The six accused were tried in the Roman forum, and all six confessed. Perpetua's father again tried to persuade his daughter to give up her faith, but was beaten down with a rod on the orders of the Roman procurator.

Perpetua, Felicitas and their fellow Christians were condemned to fight wild beasts during the games to celebrate the birthday of Geta, son of Septimius. They accepted their fate, but under Roman law Felicitas could not be killed before she had given birth. Idealistic, faithful and committed to her companions, Felicitas was concerned that her own martyrdom would be postponed because of her pregnancy. The baby, however, was born just before the games, and the six martyrs faced their death together.

Witness descriptions recount how Felicitas marched rejoicing into the amphitheatre. A wild cow savaged the women, and the guards were then ordered to cut their throats. When a novice guard failed in his job, clear-headed and courageous, Perpetua took the blade and put it into her own neck. She died having pulled her torn gown together over her thigh, to make herself appropriately modest. She, like Felicitas, was a mother who chose to die for her God rather than live for her child.

The story reminds us that a rose's name may provide intrigue far deeper than it first appears. Unusually, 'Félicité-Perpétue' honours not only nine-teenth-century French twins, but courageous women from earliest times.

FOLLOWING PAGE

The Christians Thrown to the Beasts by the Romans (nineteenth century) by Louis Félix Leullier (1811–82) illuminates the dreadful fate of Felicitas and Perpetua at the hands of the Roman senate.

The rose 'Félicité-Perpétue'

Type of rose: *Sempervirens* x Noisette
Introduced: 1827
Breeder: Jacques, Orléans, France
Parentage: Unknown

'Félicité-Perpétue' is a rose that survives neglect, and is never to be forgotten once seen in full flower. Its pale-blush pompom blooms, small but very full and quilled, are borne in clusters that completely cover the plant. To me, its most endearing quality is its scent – a heady musk fragrance, although it has been described by others as primrose.

Vigorous and wonderfully healthy, 'Félicité-Perpétue' can be seen growing abandoned in hedges, among ruins and freely wandering country gardens. In our climate she is relatively evergreen, with shiny, dark, small leaves that are plum-coloured when young. Leave her to ramble abundantly unattended over walls and trees and she will reward you handsomely. Even the wild beasts of Carthage would have been ensnared by her. Jacques always described this rose with a hyphen between its names, never "et".

Rosamund de Clifford

c.1140–1176

Many legends surround Rosamund, the beautiful mistress of King Henry II of England, and how the flower we know today as *Rosa mundi* – the "rose of the world" – came by its name. In the version most often repeated, it is whispered that Henry's queen, Eleanor of Aquitaine, assassinated her younger rival.

According to the story, Eleanor, who was known for her shrewd and cunning personality, and as a woman of great rank and privilege in her own right, approached Rosamund in the maze that Henry had built to hide his paramour at the royal palace of Woodstock. She is said to have offered Rosamund the choice between an exit from the world by poison or death by the knife. Confronted by the angry and powerful queen, Rosamund, it is said, chose to take poison.

On hearing of the death of his love, the grief-stricken Henry picked the pretty striped rose growing nearby in the hedgerows and ordered that it be named after his fair Rosamund. Each year, on the anniversary of her death, her grave was to be covered with the blossoms.

It is a wonderful, irresistible and romantic legend, but it is just that. In fact, there is no proof that there was ever a maze at Woodstock: rather, its hedgerows and paths appear to have been constructed in the imaginations of writers such as Thomas Delaney, who, in his sixteenth-century verse "The Ballad of Fair Rosamund", portrayed Rosamund as young, virtuous and misused. Delaney says of her: "A sweeter creature in this world/Could never a prince embrace." The tale was told through the centuries, and poets and writers of the Romantic era, such as Algernon Swinburne and Alfred, Lord Tennyson, did not distinguish the history from the myth.

The real Rosamund was the daughter of the Anglo-Norman knight Sir Walter de Clifford, and became Henry II's mistress around 1165, perhaps first meeting at her father's stronghold of Bredelais on the Welsh border. According to Henry's chaplain, the chronicler Giraldus Cambrensis, also known as Gerald of Wales, Rosamund was very young when she and the King began their affair. But dates for her birth vary, and if she was born around 1140, Rosamund would in fact have been in her mid twenties. The relationship was serious and it endured, remaining secret for nearly ten

A detail from *Fair Rosamund in her Bower* (c.1854) by William Bell Scott (1811–90).

years, although it is uncertain how much Rosamund would have seen of her king, as he was away from England for much of that time.

When Henry II publicly acknowledged Rosamund in 1174, Gerald of Wales made clear his disapproval: "The King, who has long been a secret adulterer, now blatantly flaunted his paramour for all to see, not a rose of the world (*rosa mundi*) as some vain and foolish people called her, but a rose of unchastity (*rosa immundi*). And since the world copies a King, he offended not only by his behaviour but even more by his bad example."

Contrary to the legend, historical documentation reveals that when Henry and Rosamund's affair became public, the formidable Eleanor of Aquitaine was securely imprisoned, with no access to the outside world. For the next fifteen years, the Queen was held in custody in a number of locations, accused of inciting her sons in open rebellion against her husband. She had acted against him not so much for his infidelity, but for his attempts to deny her rights to her lands and titles.

Some time between 1174 and 1176, Rosamund retired to a nunnery at Godstow, just outside Oxford, perhaps because she repented her affair, or more likely because of ill health. When she died, in 1176, the King and the de Cliffords buried her in grand style in a beautifully decorated tomb, placed before the high altar in Godstow Abbey. But after protests in 1191 from Bishop Hugh of Lincoln, who called Rosamund an adulteress, the body was later re-interred in the cemetery of the nuns' chapterhouse. Her new resting place bore an unfortunate and churlish inscription, noted by Ranulf Higden, a fourteenth-century monk and chronicler from Chester:

"Hic jacet in tumba rosa mundi, non rosa munda;
Non redolet, sed olet, quae redolere solet."

"Here lies the rose of the world, not a clean rose;
She no longer smells rosy, so hold your nose."

The rose Rosa mundi

Type of rose: Gallica
Introduced: Before the sixteenth century
Parentage: Sport of *Rosa gallica Officinalis*.
Other names: *Rosa gallica* 'Versicolor'

A truly striking rose, with subtle shades of crimson and ivory, its blooms do not have the brashness of many modern striped roses, but a simple, heart-stopping beauty that still endures. The flowers are like silk that has been delicately brushed and splashed with deep pink dyes. Rosa mundi produces fat buds that develop into single blooms lit up with a crown of golden stamens. She is once-flowering, but will continue over a long period, so should not be penalised for that. In our garden, she carries on through the New Zealand Christmas period.

Her leaves are small, round, and light green; the stems are thornless, although prone to being weighed down by the blooms. She is a low-growing bush and makes an ideal low hedge. This rose will tolerate the poorest of soils, and suckers well to form a good clump when grown on its own roots.

The true origins of Rosa mundi have been lost in time. Along with its parent, Rosa gallica Officinalis, the Apothecary Rose, it is one of the oldest and best-known Gallicas. The Apothecary Rose became the centre of a thriving perfume and rose petal industry in Provins, near Paris. The famed French breeder Jean-Pierre Vibert became one of the biggest producers of Gallica roses in the early nineteenth century.

Rosa gallica Officinalis was the first known rose to produce a striped sport, or natural genetic mutation on the same plant, and Rosa gallica 'Versicolor' – named Rosa mundi in England – would have been a sensation. It is thought that this crimson-splashed rose was brought into the country from the Middle East by the Crusaders, making it a much earlier introduction than its sixteenth-century recorded date.

essire Charles
de bloiie se tra
 y ure le chas
tel damoy et
lassieta lui et
ses gens plusieurs foie le fyst
assaillir et escarminchier mais
ceulz de dedens se deffendi

rent moult vaillamment car
ilz estoient enuiron deux cens
compaignons habilles et le
ther et auec deux cheualiers
du pais vaillans hommes
et hardis qui en estoient
capitaines. Dautre part
sied la bonne ville de dinid

Jeanne de Montfort

c.1295–1374

The tyranny of war and the ravages of the Black Death during the calamitous fourteenth century claimed many heroes and heroines. Among them was the fiery Jeanne, wife of Jean de Montfort.

Jeanne, who is sometimes called Joanna of Flanders after her grandfather's domain, was the daughter of Louis, Comte de Nevers and Jeanne de Rethel. In 1329 she married Jean, Comte de Montfort, who, after his half-brother's death in 1341, was one of two claimants to the ducal crown of Brittany. During the Breton war of succession (1341–1364), Jeanne de Montfort became a headstrong warrior woman and, in the early 1340s, it was a war of the Jeannes, as she pitted herself against Jeanne de Penthièvre, daughter of the old duke's younger brother. Jeanne de Penthièvre had assumed rule of Brittany with her husband, the ascetic Charles de Blois.

Jeanne de Penthièvre's backing came from the major French nobles. The de Montforts were supported by minor nobility, some bishops and most of the people; they also had an ally in Edward III of England.

In November 1341, following his surrender in the siege of Nantes, Jean de Montfort was captured by the French and imprisoned in Paris. His cause was taken up by his wife, the implacable Jeanne, with: "the courage of a man and the heart of a lion", according to the medieval chronicler, Jean Froissart. Jeanne stood with their infant son in her arms, and exhorted the de Montforts' supporters to rally and fight for their young heir. She led her husband's army into the countryside to seek reinforcements, gathering men and arms from town to town as she rode, fortifying garrisons and financing the soldiers' wages.

Jeanne was at the forefront of the heroic defence of the strategically important town of Hennebont, where she had moved her headquarters. Besieged by Charles de Blois, she inspired the townswomen of Hennebont to mobilise in defence of the ramparts with makeshift missiles. At the head of the de Montfort forces, she rode out in full armour with three hundred horsemen, directing the battle with the tactical intelligence of a seasoned general. Her raid on Charles de Blois's camp, setting fire to his quarters, earned her the name of *"La Flamme"* (The Flame).

This page from 'Chronicles of England' by Jean de Wavrin (c.1400–c.1474) shows Jeanne de Montfort and the women of Hennebont as the vessels of Charles de Blois's army arrive to beseige their town in 1342.

The way back barred, she went on to the town of Brest. In Froissart's telling of the events: "The countess did so much at Brest that she gat together five hundred spears, and then about midnight she departed from Brest, and by the sunrising she came along by the one side of the host, and came to one of the gates of Hennebont, the which was opened for her, and therein she entered and all her company with great noise of trumpets." Strengthened by these fresh troops, Hennebont held out until the English ships arrived.

In 1343, when a brief treaty marked a break in the hostilities, the Comte de Montfort was released and Jeanne sailed with their son, also called Jean, to England to seek the support and refuge of Edward III. Her husband tried to revive the fortunes of the de Montfort cause, which was then faltering, but died in 1345.

The war of succession lasted until 1364, when the young Jean, having returned to France, crushed the remnants of Jeanne de Penthièvre's army with the help of the English. Charles de Blois was killed in the battle beneath the ramparts of Auray. Peace finally came to Brittany in 1365, when Jeanne's son, under the guardianship of King Edward III of England, was crowned as Jean IV, Duc de Bretagne.

Despite her reputation as a noble fighter, Jeanne de Montfort is said to have suffered a rather ignoble end. Broken and apparently insane, she was confined in England from the mid 1340s at Tickhill castle in Yorkshire, living there for thirty years.

The rose 'Jeanne de Montfort'

Type of rose: Moss
Introduced: 1851
Breeder: Robert, Angers, France
Parentage: Unknown

'Jeanne de Montfort' is one of the more vigorous of the Moss roses and grows to a tall shrub or small climber if given her head. Like her headstrong namesake,

her tough stems are well armed, with bronzy moss and fierce prickles that set off the slightly glossy, mid-green leaves.

She produces large clusters of warm pink flowers from tight little buds that have long sepals with a substantial covering of brown moss. Her blooms are slightly less than fully double and, when open, display bright yellow stamens. The flowers are sweetly scented. This is an excellent rose that should be better known.

Many of the Moss roses from the nineteenth-century French gardener and rose breeder Robert were named after celebrated French women and men. Both Jeanne de Montfort and Marie de Blois (see pp.38–41), after whom it is thought Robert named another of his roses, lived within two centuries of one another, and both had associations with the Blois estate and the Orléans family.

Robert is known to us only by his surname, or as Monsieur Robert.

He was gardener to Jean Pierre Vibert, another notable and prolific breeder. He bought Vibert's nursery in 1850 and thereafter founded the breeding dynasty of Moreau-Robert. The dynasty specialised in breeding Moss roses, reaching its peak between 1850 and 1890 and producing one hundred and fifty different Moss varieties. Moss roses declined in popularity at the end of the nineteenth century and few are commercially available today.

esse du saint
esperit pour nos
excellente et

Yolande d'Aragon

c.1380–1442

The formidable Yolande d'Aragon, "Queen of the Four Kingdoms" and Duchesse d'Anjou, was for more than forty years a pivotal figure in the history of fifteenth-century Europe. But her genius and influence have remained relatively unappreciated; eclipsed, perhaps, by the woman she championed – the young Jeanne d'Arc.

As the daughter of King Juan I of Aragon and Yolande de Bar, Yolande was powerful in her own right, and in 1400 she married Louis II, Duc d'Anjou, King of Naples and Sicily, adding to her titles. She was considered wise and intelligent, with a talent for politics and nose for intrigue. The couple had five children, and their daughter Marie was to become a future Queen Consort of France.

Louis spent much time away at war, leaving his wife to rule Anjou and Provence and protect their children's future. His death left Yolande a widow in her thirties, but she took control of the house of Anjou as regent for their son Louis III, defending it against attack from the English during the Hundred Years' War. She further secured her family's fortune when she arranged the marriage of Marie to Charles VII of the House of Valois. This alliance prompted Yolande's personal involvement in the survival of the Valois dynasty as rulers of France and her association with Jeanne d'Arc.

Charles's father, King Charles VI, suffered from periods of madness and delusion, leaving a power vacuum that brought feuds and conflicts as different factions fought for control of France. Charles was the King's fifth son, but became dauphin, or heir, in 1417 following the early deaths of his older brothers. Yolande had taken Charles into her care at the court in Angers, protecting him from the many plots on his life and acting as a mother to the young man. His real mother, Queen Isabeau, opposed her son and his supporters and, in 1420, allied herself with the English under King Henry V. Yolande ensured her prospective son-in-law's safety and, in his cause, worked against his mother, who would ultimately denounce Charles as illegitimate.

Yolande put her considerable resources – both intellectual and financial – into his campaign, and refused to return him to Isabeau. According

Yolande d'Aragon and her children kneeling before an image of the Virgin Mary and the Christ child from *Book of Oaths and Book of the Foundation of the Royal Chapel of Gué de Maulny* (fourteenth to seventeenth centuries).

to sources quoted by twentieth-century writer Jehanne d'Orliac in her book *Yolande d'Anjou*, Yolande told Isabeau: "We have not nurtured and cherished this one for you to make him die like his brothers or go mad like his father, or become English like you. I keep him for my own. Come and take him away if you dare." In 1422, the year of Charles VI's death, the Dauphin married Marie.

However, it was Yolande's early support of Jeanne d'Arc that ensured her place in history, as she played a crucial part in orchestrating Jeanne's appearance on the French political stage as the saviour of the King.

Yolande prepared Jeanne d'Arc as God's emissary, thrusting her into the forefront of the campaign to have Charles crowned as ruler of France. She was in charge of one of the examinations of Jeanne to prove her purity, and it was recorded that: "She and [her] ladies found that she was certainly a true and entire maid, in whom could be found no corruption nor mark of violence." Jeanne also stayed with one of Yolande's trusted counsellors as preparations were made for her role in the war against the English. However, after Charles VII was crowned in 1429, he and Yolande did nothing to save Jeanne d'Arc when she was captured and handed over to face her martyrdom.

Yolande d'Aragon was a formidable and powerful influence in the first half of the fifteenth century. She was an expert in the art of practical and pragmatic politics, making use of mistresses and informers in her campaigns. Her backing of Jeanne d'Arc was a tour de force in the battle to bring stability to France and have her son-in-law Charles VII legitimised as king. Yolande's grandson King Louis XI of France praised her strength of will and character. She had, he said: "A man's heart in a woman's body."

The rose 'Yolande d'Aragon'

Type of rose: Hybrid Perpetual (but sometimes described as a Portland)
Introduced: 1843
Breeder: Vibert, Angers, France
Parentage: Unknown

This rose is as beautiful as Yolande herself. She has flat, double, especially large blooms borne in clusters on an upright bush. The quartered blooms vary in colour from clear rose pink to purplish mauve – a delightful muddle with a heavenly fragrance that is described as "lingering and haunting".

The healthy, strong bush has light green, matte, plentiful and luxuriant foliage. Given a little summer care, good water and food, this rose will repeat flower in the autumn. Although she closely resembles a Gallica, and was bred by the master of Gallicas, 'Yolande d'Aragon' is sometimes classified as a Perpetual Damask or Portland.

Jean Pierre Vibert grew up in Paris during the Revolution and the Reign of Terror, but in 1839 settled in the rose-growing area of Anjou – the seat of Yolande's power base. Along with the rose 'Jeanne d'Arc', Vibert, with his protégé Robert, created sumptuous roses to celebrate many of the all-powerful rulers of this region from four centuries before. Although he is best known for his Gallicas, Vibert was a prolific breeder of many of the old rose families. He died in 1866 aged eighty-nine, leaving a legacy of sensual roses. A contemporary of his commented: "We should wreath his tomb with our homage and our respect."

Jeanne d'Arc

c. 1412–1431

Jeanne d'Arc, the Maid of Orléans – or simply *"La Pucelle"* (The Maid) – has been a source of inspiration through the centuries. Iconic images show the seventeen-year-old girl clad in armour and sometimes riding on a white horse, sword in hand, leading the army of the Dauphin Charles VII into battle. Jeanne became a symbol of French unity and courage, and remains a source of national pride in France to this day.

According to historical accounts, Jeanne was born in the village of Domrémy (now Domrémy-La-Pucelle) on the north-eastern frontier of France, the illiterate daughter of a farmer and local official. Her birth came during the Hundred Years' War, a series of wars fought between England and France for control of the French throne. In 1420, the Treaty of Troyes handed over much of France to the English king, Henry V, who was supported by the Burgundians.

What we know of Jeanne's early life comes largely from two sets of documents: the records of Jeanne's Trial of Condemnation in 1431 and of the Trial of Rehabilitation begun in 1450. These include Jeanne's own account of her life. It would seem that, as a girl, she learned traditional female crafts such as sewing and spinning, but was also adept at the plough, working crops and tending the animals.

At the age of thirteen, she began to hear mysterious voices, which she claimed to be messages from God. "She heard the voice upon the right side, towards the church, and she rarely heard it without an accompanying brightness … And, after she had heard this voice upon three occasions, she understood that it was the voice of an angel," recounts the chronicler Enguerrand de Mostrelet.

Jeanne identified the speaker as St Michael, and also described being visited by visions of St Catherine and St Margaret. She became convinced that these voices were telling her it was her duty to drive the English from France and have the Dauphin crowned king at Reims. Although Charles VII's father was dead, so that he was nominally king, he ruled only south of the Loire valley. Jeanne always referred to him as the "dauphin", or heir, and insisted that, to be truly sovereign of France, he must be crowned and anointed in Reims, where all French kings were traditionally consecrated.

Clad in armour and clutching her sword, Jeanne d'Arc kneels in prayer in this detail from *Joan of Arc* (1865) by Sir John Everett Millais (1829–96).

By 1427, Charles VII's situation had become grave. Reims, to the east of Paris, was held by his enemies and the English were besieging Orléans, south of the French capital on the river Loire; this the last strategically placed city that was loyal to his cause.

In February 1429, with the help of Robert de Baudricourt, captain of the nearby town of Vaucouleurs, Jeanne arrived at Charles VII's court at Chinon in the Loire valley. Charles was at first reluctant to grant her an audience, but after two days he agreed to see her. A test was set for Jeanne, according to accounts of this first meeting: she was introduced to several other men, and told they were the King, while the real Charles stood behind his courtiers. Jeanne identified him straightaway.

Charles did not know what to make of this young woman's extraordinary request to lead his army, or of her claim to be a divine envoy. "Gentle Dauphin, my name is Joan the Maid and the King of the Heavens informs you, through me, that you will be consecrated and crowned in the town of

The rose 'Jeanne d'Arc'

Type of rose: Alba
Introduced: 1818
Breeder: Vibert, Angers, France
Parentage: Seedling of 'Belle Elisa'

The country girl, soldier and saint from Domrémy had three roses named after her. This one, the Alba, is the most famous and the only one known to be grown today. The others are a Noisette (Verdier 1848) and a Polyantha (Levavasseur 1909).

'Jeanne d'Arc' has rich, creamy buds that open to a virginal white. The blooms are medium sized with muddled centres, and with a rich, sweet, powerful perfume. Arriving in late spring, they ease the eye after the vibrant hues of the earlier-flowering Gallicas.

She is clothed in a mass of leaden blue-green, matte foliage and grows straight and tall, proudly reaching for her God. She is well armed and travels freely through our garden. The foliage contrasts
rather well with the creamy buds and startling white blooms.

The Alba roses are a select family, which reign supreme over other once-flowering varieties. They have vigour, health, longevity and a sense of purity about them that charms the gardener. They will soften a border, give weight and height to it and create interest after blooming because of the grey or blue-tinged leaves. The canes arch gracefully when laden with blooms.

Jean Pierre Vibert was a shoemaker from Angers who became one of the first growers in France, after Jacques-Louis Descemet (1761–1839), to cultivate roses commercially. He was one of the period's most respected rose breeders and many of his creations still flourish today.

Reims", Jeanne told Charles, according to the testimony of her confessor, Father Jean Pasquerel. Unsure whether she was deluded, a fraud or truly carrying out God's will, Charles had her examined by an ecclesiastical commission, and her virginity verified by his mother-in-law and protector Yolande d'Aragon. Jeanne was convincing in her faith and sincerity, and the commission advised Charles to accept her offer.

He had a full suit of armour made for her, and she was given a squire and servants. With her standard of white, bearing the image of Christ in judgement, with angels and a white dove, in April 1429 Jeanne rode forth to besieged Orléans at the head of the King's army.

Inspired by her passion, the French changed their tactics and took fort after fort until the English finally retreated from the city, lifting the siege on 8 May. It is said that Jeanne was greatly skilled as a horsewoman and in combat, handling a tilting lance with power. During one battle, she was injured by an arrow, but returned to lead the final attack. News of her heroism and her divine mission spread; French morale rose, while the English were gripped with a superstitious dread of the "witch".

After Orléans, Jeanne and the French army took more towns along the Loire before they inflicted a crushing defeat on the English at Patay on 18 June. Charles was crowned and anointed as King of France on 17 July 1429, with the Maid and her standard at his side. Jeanne's work was done.

However, she continued to fight on in the name of the King. Jeanne was finally captured by the Burgundians during a skirmish at Compiègne in May 1430, and later handed over to the English. By this time she was the heroine of all France but, to his lasting shame, Charles VII made no attempt to secure her release. Jeanne was tried as a heretic by a church court, and questioned from February 1431 for nearly a month. The records of her trial show how she confounded her interrogators with her subtle answers regarding her faith.

She was condemned and, after a period in which she appeared to recant, sent to be to burned at the stake in the market square of Rouen. One account describes how she requested a cross from the church so she could have it continually before her until she died. It was 30 May 1431, and less than two-and-a-half years had passed since she had set out on her mission to free France.

Two decades after her capture, Charles VII ordered a retrial, which declared Jeanne innocent, and in 1920 she was canonised as a saint by the Catholic Church.

Marie, Comtesse de Blois

c. 1426–1486

S everal women during the twelfth to fifteenth centuries were known by the name of Marie de Blois. Of these, the fourteen-year-old wife of the courtly poet, Charles, Duc d'Orléans, is the perfect candidate to have had this full-flowered pink rose named after her.

Marie lived during a confused and bloody period of French history, the era of Jeanne d'Arc and the Hundred Years' War between England and France, and of the conflict between the Armagnac and Burgundian factions of the French nobility. She was born Marie von Kleve, the daughter of Adolph von Kleve and Marie de Bourgogne, and the niece of Philippe le Bon, Duc de Bourgogne.

Her future husband inherited the title of Duc d'Orléans just before his thirteenth birthday, after his father's brutal assassination in 1407. He became one of the leaders of the Armagnac cause, but was captured following the brutal Battle of Agincourt (25 October 1415) and imprisoned in England. He remained there for twenty-five years, a crucial and valuable pawn in the turmoil between England and France.

Relations between the families of Marie and Charles were complex. Charles supported his half-brother Jean, Comte de Dunois, in protecting the Orléans territories while he was held hostage. Dunois fought alongside Jeanne d'Arc as she took up the cause of Orléans and France to free them from the English, while it was Philippe's forces who captured Jeanne in 1430. However, ten years later, Philippe and his wife, Isabella of Portugal, were instrumental in arranging Charles's release, Isabella collecting funds from the French nobility to pay his ransom to the English.

Marie and Charles were married on 27 November 1440, shortly after his release from captivity. Rather than taking a central role in French politics, Charles retired with his new wife to the Château de Blois, between Troyes and Orléans on the river Loire. One of Charles's titles was Comte de Blois, making Marie the Comtesse.

In Blois they surrounded themselves with writers, artists and architects, with plays, banquets, juggling and minstrels. The château, nestled in the ancient town, ranks as one of the more splendid castles of the Loire, with buildings representing the great periods of French architecture from

The poet Charles d'Orléans with his wife Marie in the castle at Blois in a painting of 1845 by Ange François (1800–1872).

Gothic to Classical. It was enlarged over several centuries and by many owners, but Marie and Charles began the project of restoration and aggrandisement, demolishing the old fortress and rebuilding in stone and brick, and commissioning the château's galleries and magnificent staircase.

They turned Blois into a literary centre reminiscent of Charles's childhood among the Loire châteaux, surrounded not only by luxury, but by learning and culture. The Duc was interested in philosophy, science and theology – interests he passed on to his wife. He had spent his captivity in England writing, producing about five hundred poems, and was considered one of the foremost romantic poets of the Middle Ages. Marie also took an active role in literary life. She, too, wrote poetry and collected books, the inventory of her library revealing a select but impressive collection. Scholars have suggested that two poems in a compilation of Charles's work, with the name "Madame d'Orléans" beside the title, were possibly written by Marie. An elegant rondel, or rondeau, based, perhaps, on the more famous poem by Charles with which it shares a first line, begins:

"En la forest de longue actente,
Entrée suis en une sente,
Dont oster je ne puis mon cueur,
Pourquoy je viz en grant langueur
Par Fortune qui me tourmente.
Souvent Espoir chascun contente,
Excepté moy, povre dolente,
Qui, nuyt et jour, suis en doleur."

"Where Hope offers others consolation,
She has left me, piteous and mournful,
To lament through night and day.
In the forest of deep longing,
I followed along a path,
From which I cannot wrench my heart,
So I live in great weariness
As Fortune torments me."

Charles was forty-six when he married Marie; she was his third wife, his first having died when he was still an adolescent and his second while he was held in England. Accounts suggest Marie and Charles had a peaceful marriage; it endured for twenty-five years, until Charles's death.

Their first surviving child, a daughter also named Marie, was not born until Marie de Blois was in her early thirties. There followed a son, the future King Louis XII of France, and another daughter, Anne, born in 1464, the year before her father's death. Not yet forty when Charles died, Marie de Blois is thought to have later secretly married a courtier.

A magnificent tapestry hangs in the Musée des Arts Décoratifs in Paris, showing Charles and Marie amid the splendour of muses. Produced in Brussels and dating from the fifteenth century, its details of flowers, robes and angels' wings are worked in wool and silk. In a time of great conflict, Marie's legacy is a life imbued with gentleness, beauty and poetry.

The rose 'Marie de Blois'

Type of rose: Moss
Introduced: 1852
Breeder: Robert, Angers, France
Parentage: Unknown

This dense, tallish-growing rose is a delightfully free-flowering gem. Its blooms form randomly placed clusters of bright pink that are heavily fragrant, globular and frilled. 'Marie de Blois' is generous with her full, luscious blooms.

The reddish moss, which covers the buds in this family, often raises the eyebrows of non-rosarians visiting our gardens, who suspect that we have, in our non-spray régime, an infestation of aphids. Not so. The characteristic mossing is an interesting curiosity, which has survived the fashions of the rose-loving public. The mossed, sticky buds, when lightly brushed, smell of turpentine – which, surprisingly, is not at all unpleasant.

The leaves of this rose are bright green, with characteristic reddish tones on the margins of the new foliage. The growth habit is bushy and vigorous on a shapely plant, which is suitable for hedging.

'Marie de Blois' demands recognition as a good example of a small family of roses. Moss roses are natural mutations from the Centifolia family, with an aromatic, resinous moss covering the stem, calyx, sepals and leaflets of the flower.

The rose was released some four centuries after our Marie de Blois lived. The breeder, Robert, named many of his roses after interesting French women – he also created the roses 'Mme de Sombreuil' (see p.85) and 'Jeanne de Montfort' (see p.27). His mentor, Vibert, was the breeder of 'Jeanne d'Arc' (see pp.34–5), and it is this interest in the affairs of Orléans in the fifteenth century that leads me to believe that Robert was commemorating the wife of Charles d'Orléans with his rose.

Amy Robsart

1532–1560

This charming young woman was to become the central figure in an Elizabethan political mystery whose power to intrigue has stretched through the centuries. Her early death caused a scandal, the web of suspicions spreading to Amy's husband, Robert Dudley, his liaison with Queen Elizabeth I of England and his enemies at court.

Amy was the only legitimate daughter of Sir John Robsart, Sheriff of Norfolk and Suffolk. In 1550, she married Robert Dudley, the future Earl of Leicester, just before her eighteenth birthday, when Robert was also seventeen. Their wedding was held at the royal palace of Sheen, in Surrey, and King Edward VI, Elizabeth's half-brother, was among the guests. Their union was a love-match, a fact suggested by William Cecil, the leading Elizabethan statesman, when he later wrote: "*Nuptiae carnales a laetitia incipient et in luctu terminantur,*" or: "Carnal marriages begin with happiness and end in grief." The young couple depended financially on their fathers, but evidence suggests the marriage had started well enough, until Robert became ambitious, interested in matters of state and as a consequence neglectful of his wife.

Following the death of Edward VI, Robert's father, the Duke of Northumberland, was involved in the attempt to establish Lady Jane Grey, wife of one of his younger sons, on the throne of England. When the conspiracy failed, Robert was one of the Dudley family members tried for high treason. He was imprisoned in the Tower of London, where Amy visited him, and was sentenced to death in early 1554. However, Robert had influential friends and was released and pardoned a little over a year later. He and the Princess Elizabeth were childhood friends who had been educated together and, as his prestige grew, Robert was absent for long periods of time, attending her business. When Elizabeth I was crowned in 1558, she made him her Master of the Horse; by 1559 it was clear that he was a royal favourite. Amy, meanwhile, tended to the estates bequeathed to them by her father; it was not usual for wives to accompany their husbands to court.

There was no family to keep her occupied, and no evidence that Amy became pregnant. Any isolation she may have felt would have certainly been aggravated by the news from court of her husband's relationship with

A portrait of Amy Robsart (1884) by William Frederick Yeames (1835–1918).

the Queen. The Spanish ambassador, the Count de Feria, wrote: "It is said that her Majesty visits him in his chamber day and night. People talk of this so freely that they go on to say that his wife has a malady of the breast and the Queen is only waiting for her to die to marry Lord Robert."

Amy moved between their houses until she decided to live at Cumnor Place in Oxfordshire. She kept to herself there, possibly mindful of the court gossip. Meanwhile, Dudley was "preparing to divorce his wife", according to the Spanish ambassador's letters to his own monarch, so that he would be better situated with the new Queen. The court of Queen Elizabeth I was a hotbed of intrigue, with members of her court aligning themselves with the various suitors for her hand in marriage. Lord Robert's enemies prepared to entrap him with rumours about his desire to kill his wife. But did he or they have any part in her death, or was it a tragic accident?

On Sunday 8 September 1560, Amy was found lying dead at the bottom of her stairs, with a broken neck. Her household was away at the local fair in Abingdon, on her orders, and she was alone. Dudley heard the news while staying with the Queen at Windsor, but he did not go personally to find out what had happened, or attend her funeral. Instead, he sent Sir Thomas Blount, his steward, and called for a full investigation.

The inquest jury returned a verdict of accidental death, and no evidence was ever found linking what happened to Dudley. The "malady of the breast" referred to by the Spanish ambassador is today thought to have been breast cancer, which, it is supposed, made Amy's spine fragile so that she was susceptible to stumbling or falling. There is also a suspicion that she was depressed at her husband's infidelity; as her maid, Mrs Picto, told Blount, she heard her: "Pray to God to deliver her from desperation."

Rumours continued to plague Dudley from all over Britain. Mary Queen of Scots was reputed to have said of her cousin: "The Queen of England is going to marry her horsekeeper, who has killed his wife to make room for her." In fact, whether it was murder, accident or suicide, Amy's death effectively prevented him from marrying his queen, and the suspicion about his part in it remained with him. Poor Amy was buried with pomp and ceremony at Oxford.

Amy Robsart and her husband Robert Dudley, Earl of Leicester, (c.1827) at Cumnor Place, Oxfordshire, by Richard Parkes Bonington (1802–28).

The rose 'Amy Robsart'

Type of rose: Sweet Briar Hybrid
Introduced: 1894
Breeder: Lord Penzance (introduced by
Keynes, Williams and Co, England)
Parentage: *Rosa eglanteria* (alternatively
called *R. rubiginosa*) x unknown Hybrid
Perpetual or Bourbon

*One of the few remaining Penzance
hybrids, 'Amy Robsart' still survives
as an attractive and vigorous member
of this small, elite family. She is an
abundant bloomer bearing flowers of
deep rose pink, large and semi-double,
with the exposed stamens adding to
her beauty when fully open. She is
spectacular when in full bloom, so
can be forgiven for appearing a little
dull for the rest of the year.*

*Her flowers are sweetly scented, and
her foliage just slightly so, with that
delightful sweet briar, green apple
fragrance. An added benefit is the lovely
scarlet hips, which compensate for the
lack of flowers in late summer.*

*This rose forms a sprawling shrub that
will spread to two-and-a-half metres and
tolerates shade, so it will do well in the
back of a border. She is vigorous and
healthy, not at all like her tragic and frail
namesake. Although Lord Penzance's
roses are fairly uniform, with similar
breeding, they are all healthy and
vigorous, making a magnificent show in
midsummer. Of his sixteen hybrid roses
only a few remain commercially
available. We are lucky to have enjoyed
three of them in our own gardens.*

MARIE
REINE
DESCOS
SE

Mary Stuart, Queen of Scots

1542–1587

B orn one week before the untimely death of her father, the Scottish King James V, Mary Stuart was crowned Queen of Scotland at less than a year old. Her life was destined to be a stormy one, bedevilled by intrigues and treachery spanning three countries and three crowns, and embroiled in the inter-religious wars between Protestants and Catholics, English and Scots.

Mary was a daughter of the Auld Alliance between Scotland and France. Her mother was Marie de Guise, an aristocrat from Lorraine, born into the House of Bourbon. But Mary was also of interest to the English King Henry VIII, who tried, first by diplomacy and then by force, to secure a marriage between her and his son, Prince Edward, later Edward VI. In 1543, the Treaty of Greenwich agreed a peace between Scotland and England, and Mary's betrothal. The Scots, however, changed their minds, partly because Henry VIII demanded that Mary be sent immediately to spend her childhood in England.

With the English army attacking the Scottish Borders, burning, looting and killing, Scotland turned for help to its Auld Alliance partner. France sent troops, and a new marriage was agreed for Mary: with the Dauphin François, son of the recently crowned French King Henri II. At the age of five, Mary set sail from Dumbarton on the west coast of Scotland and travelled to the royal château of St-Germain-en-Laye, near Paris. At the French court, Mary grew up well educated, refined, tall and beautiful, but she was challenged by frail health all her life.

It seems that the young Mary quickly won the heart of the Dauphin; from their first meeting in 1548, watched anxiously by the court, they became friends, sharing secrets and seeking each other's company. They wed in 1558, when Mary was fifteen and François fourteen. Part of the marriage contract was a secret treaty that, if Mary died childless, her claims to the thrones of Scotland and England would pass to the Catholic French crown. Henri II made sure that when Edward's half-sister, the Catholic Queen Mary I, died, Mary Stuart claimed that she, not her Protestant cousin Elizabeth I, was the rightful Queen of England. This act would always put Mary and Elizabeth in opposition.

A detail from a miniature of Mary Queen of Scots (c.1560) by a follower of François Clouet (c.1510–72).

The death of King Henri II in 1559 meant that François became King François II, and Mary became Queen Consort of France. But, less than eighteen months later, she was widowed when her husband died from an ear infection. In a poem Mary wrote:

"By day, by night, I think of him
In wood or mead, or where I be
My heart keeps watch for one who's gone
And I feel he's aye with me."

Banished by her mother-in-law, Catherine de Medici, she returned to Scotland at the age of eighteen to face the powerful Protestant Reformation movement and a country torn by religious strife and inter-clan rivalry. She was a pawn in the ambitions of both Elizabeth and the Scottish nobility, and was no match for their cunning and double-dealing. Catholic Mary attempted reconciliation with her cousin, but with only limited success.

Mary was a tolerant and popular monarch in Scotland, but her three marriages were disasters. She described her second husband, Henry Stuart, Lord Darnley, as: "The lustiest and best-proportioned lang man" she had met. But Darnley was arrogant, politically inept and a frequenter of taverns. He was also a Catholic, placing another barrier between Mary and Elizabeth, and rousing the rebellion of the Protestant Scottish nobles.

Mary drew close instead to her private secretary, Davide Rizzio. Jealous of Rizzio's political influence, Darnley wanted more power than Mary would give him. With a group of nobles, he arranged for Rizzio to be murdered in the Queen's chambers at Holyrood Palace in Edinburgh, in front of the pregnant Mary. Three months later, she gave birth to Darnley's son, who would become James VI of Scotland and James I of England. Mary persuaded Darnley to give up his collaborators but she never forgave him.

On 10 February 1567, Darnley was found dead – thought strangled – after an explosion, which was probably intended to cover up his murder, destroyed the house near Glasgow where he was staying. Mary was implicated through her association with the man who was to become her third husband, the Earl of Bothwell, and through letters she had allegedly written to him. Although Mary is generally now regarded as innocent, and may even have been the intended target, the incident began her downfall.

The Earl of Bothwell, thought of by Mary as a "strong wise protector", was charged, but acquitted, after which he tricked a reluctant Mary into accompanying him to his castle at Dunbar. There, she eventually agreed to marry him, in May 1567, in the hope it would stabilise the country. According to some, Bothwell raped her to force the marriage. These intrigues brought condemnation in Scotland and across Europe, resulting in Mary's enforced separation from Bothwell and captivity at Lochleven castle, where she agreed to abdicate, making her one-year-old son James the King.

After ten months at Lochleven, Mary escaped. She mounted an abortive comeback and fled to England, arriving by ship in Cumbria on 16 May 1568. She was still only twenty-five. Mary pleaded with Elizabeth to restore her Scottish throne, but was instead held as a prisoner, as she was too much of a threat. Mary was to spend her remaining eighteen years being moved from house to house in England. During that time, the English Catholics plotted repeatedly to rescue Mary, assassinate Elizabeth and restore Catholicism to England.

In 1586, Elizabeth finally brought her cousin to trial on charges of treason, after receiving proof of Mary's entanglement in the Babington Plot against Elizabeth's life. At first, Mary refused to appear in person, saying: "I am myself a queen, the daughter of a king, a stranger and a true kinswoman of the Queen of England. I came into this kingdom under promise of assistance, and aid, against my enemies and not as a subject, instead I have been detained and imprisoned."

In the end, she realised she would have to defend herself. "Remember that the theatre of the world is wider than the realm of England," Mary said to her judges. In court, she was allowed no counsel or witnesses, but in spite of this and increasingly frail health, she acquitted herself well. Her parting words to the court of nobles were: "My Lords and gentlemen, I place my cause in the hands of God." Her cool, clever, single-handed defence against the odds can only be admired, but Mary was found guilty. Her cousin delayed over signing the death warrant, suffering torments of indecision. But eventually a ruse was devised, so that Elizabeth could sign it among a sheaf of other papers, allowing her to shirk full responsibility. On 8 February 1587, aged forty-four, Mary was publicly beheaded.

After five months lying unburied in a sealed lead coffin, she was given a royal funeral in Peterborough Cathedral. In 1612, after he had come to the English throne as James I, Mary's son moved her remains to her final resting place in Westminster Abbey.

The rose 'Mary Queen of Scots'

Type of rose: Wild rose *Rosa pimpinellifolia*
(formerly called *Rosa spinosissima*)
Other names: Scotch Rose or Burnet Rose

Tradition has it that this tough little rose was brought by Queen Mary to Scotland from France, when she returned after the death of François II. 'Mary Queen of Scots' is a lovely and somewhat unusual rose, as its plum-tinted, grey-lilac buds and opening flowers reveal a gorgeous contrast between light and dark pink shades, and golden prominent stamens. Sweetly scented, her blooms age to produce wonderful maroon-black hips.

The red-brown stems carry long, pale thorns and many tiny red bristles on the stalks. The small leaflets have round notches like fern leaves. She suckers madly, forming large clumps. Like most of the Pimpinellifolia family, she produces great autumn tones.

There is some doubt as to the authenticity of "our" Mary. Although she matches the description from Mary McMurtrie, she does differ from other descriptions. Whatever we grow as Mary, she is as tough as her namesake and spreads freely through our brick patio.

The original parent is a low-growing wild rose that colonises the highlands and lowlands of Scotland, surviving on rocky outcrops, riverbanks and coastlines. Thriving in the poorest of soils, defying sun and drought, wind and salt spray, it grows all over Europe, Siberia, Turkey and Asia. It was referenced in Gerard's "Herball" in 1597 as the Pimpinell Rose, which rosarian Graham Stuart Thomas enthuses over in his book "Shrub Roses of Today": "They are nearly as prolific of their flowers as they are of their leaves and thorns. A bush in full flower is a wonderful sight; the wiry shoots bending under the weight of the blossoms, and the whole creating a brilliant effect. Mere plenitude would not be enough, however; they fortunately have a sweet charm of their own, an exhilarating fresh scent – just like lily of the valley in its revivifying purity – and they flower in summer just when we are ready to welcome roses, before the hot days of summer bring forth the greater garden varieties."

Nur Mahal

1577–1645

Nur Mahal – "The Light of Palaces", as her adoring second husband called her – was the most powerful empress of the Mughal Dynasty, which ruled over much of the Indian subcontinent from 1526 and came to an end in the mid-nineteenth century. Her family were Persian nobility from what is today Tehran, in Iran, but their fortunes had suffered. Ghias Beg, his pregnant wife Asmat Begum and their children migrated to India, joining a caravan travelling south. In Kandahar, now in Afghanistan, Asmat gave birth to their daughter, Mehr-un-Nisaa. A number of accounts describe how the future Empress was nearly abandoned by her parents during their hazardous journey. With no money and no food, they left her, but the baby's cries drew them back.

In India, her father managed to find work at the court of the third Mughal Emperor, Akbar. There he rose quickly through the court's hierarchy, in time becoming a trusted minister and treasurer. In 1594, when Mehr-un-Nisaa was seventeen, Akbar arranged for the young woman, who was renowned for her beauty and graciousness, to be married to Sher Afghan Quli Khan, a Persian soldier of some renown. She had a child with him, a daughter who was later known as Ladli, but was widowed in 1607, when her husband was accused of plotting against Akbar's son Jahangir and executed for treason.

Mehr-un-Nisaa returned with her daughter to the Mughal court, as a lady-in-waiting to Jahangir's stepmother, Ruqaiya Begum, who also happened to be the controller of his *zenana*, the women's quarters at court. After Akbar's death in 1605, Jahangir had become Emperor, and accounts describe him as self-indulgent, weak and cruel. At the festival of Nowruz in 1611, Mehr-un-Nisaa caught his attention with her beauty, her intelligence and her singing. Mutamid Khan, Jahangir's courtier, describes how: "Since … Fate had decreed that she should be the queen of the world and the princess of the time, it happened that on the celebration of the New Year's day, in the sixth year of the Emperor's reign, her appearance caught his far-seeing eye and so captivated him that he included her among the inmates of his select harem."

This Indian painting from the Mughal period (c.1800) depicts Nur Mahal entertaining the Emperor Jahangir and his son, Shah Jahan, in one of her cherished gardens.

Jahangir, it is said, arranged to meet her in a rose garden and married her two months later, calling her Nur Mahal. She was thirty-four and possibly his twentieth wife, but she became his most favoured. Sir Thomas Roe, the British ambassador at that time, wrote in his journal of life at the Mughal court: "He hath one wife, or queen, whom he esteems and favours above all other women; and his whole empire is govern'd at this day by her counsel."

This brilliant woman, who exercised her skills in administration, politics, economics and culture, was to become the virtual ruler of India. She was adored by her husband, who was addicted to opium and alcohol, and who appears to have recognised that he needed her help to maintain both his health and his throne. Jahangir's first mention of her in his memoirs comes two years after their marriage, when he writes about his secret illness, which he had kept from everyone except his wife: "Than whom I did not think anyone was fonder of me." In 1616, he renamed her Nur Jahan, or "The Light of the World".

The rule of *purdah*, or separation and concealment of women from men, meant that Nur Mahal had to rule through trusted male relatives and ministers, among them one of her brothers, Asaf Khan, and her stepsons – although they were later to side against her. She was unable to show her face outside the *zenana*, but nevertheless it was she who ruled, giving the orders, promoting or demoting, and she who granted funds, concessions and favours. Nur Mahal is the only Mughal empress to have had coins struck with her own name. She collected duties and traded with Europeans, her business and wealth growing with her influence. This power was unprecedented in India at that time.

Nur Mahal was especially interested in the affairs of women, and supported orphaned girls by giving them land and dowries. She was in charge of the Emperor's household, which included wives, children, ladies-in-waiting, concubines, servants, eunuchs, guards, entertainers and artists. Nothing happened without her knowledge and consent, and she pushed the social and cultural conventions of her times to the limit.

Well educated and a skilled and published poet, Nur Mahal became a patron of art and architecture; she designed interiors, rugs, dresses and ornaments, and her Persian culture dominated the fashions and clothing styles of the time. She loved plants and gardens, and surrounded herself with beds of roses and irises. "If the rosebud can be opened by the breeze in the meadow, the key to our heart's lock is the beloved's smile," wrote the Empress in one of her poems.

A miniature portrait (c.1675) of Empress Nur Mahal, who was renamed Nur Jahan, "The Light of the World", by her husband Emperor Jahangir.

She assisted with the layout of many Persian gardens, including the beautiful Shalimar-Bagh on Lake Dal in Kashmir, with its terraces, fountains and a pavilion that is supported by fluted pillars of black marble. She designed her father's mausoleum at Agra, the first in India to be made from white marble, and the forerunner to the Taj Mahal, where her niece Mumtaz Mahal lies.

Jahangir's later years were marked by illness and rebellions, as the Emperor refused to name a successor. Coups were attempted by his son Shah Jahan and by his foremost general Mahabat Khan, who had turned against Nur Mahal, saying: "Never has there been a king so subject to the will of his wife." Nur Mahal gathered Jahangir's forces to quell these attempts, and tales tell of her leading her troops on an elephant, shooting arrows from behind her curtained *howdah* enclosure.

Nur Mahal's star waned after her husband's death in 1627. She was viewed with suspicion and scorn by the new administration and confined as a virtual prisoner in Lahore by the new Emperor, Shah Jahan, husband of Mumtaz Mahal.

She spent her last days living quietly with her daughter and died at the age of sixty-eight. Nur Mahal is buried at Shahdara Bagh, near Lahore in Pakistan, in a single-storey mausoleum she had built herself and decorated with floral frescoes. Her last resting place is next to her husband, who lies in the tomb she designed for him, surrounded by the fragrant gardens she delighted in.

The rose 'Nur Mahal'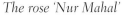

Type: Hybrid Musk
Introduced: 1923
Breeder: Pemberton, England
Parentage: *Rosa* 'Château de Clos Vougeot' x Hybrid Musk seedling

'Nur Mahal' is one of the more vibrantly coloured old roses, with the brightness so typical of Indian fabrics, crossing that boundary from the pastel, once-flowering varieties to the stronger hues of the free-flowering modern cultivars. She grows tall and clothes herself in large clusters of semi-double, bright crimson flowers that are well-perfumed with a slightly musky fragrance. She displays her showy stamens over a long flowering season with the flair of an artist.

This shrub has plentiful, dark, leathery foliage on a sturdy plant. Bred by the Reverend Joseph Pemberton, it is not widely grown today, which is a pity, because she adds a bright, flamboyant dimension to the garden when it starts to look a little tired.

The Mughal Empress Nur Mahal herself used the method devised by the ancient civilisations of Egypt, Greece and Rome to obtain attar of roses for perfume, although her husband apparently believed she had discovered the secret of distillation independently. Jack Harkness recounts the story in his book, "Roses". When Nur Mahal was being rowed along a stinking canal with her husband, he writes, she had rose petals thrown onto the water to sweeten the air. Being a clever woman, she observed an oily film on the water when the petals on it were exposed to the hot sun. So she ordered that petals from her garden be gathered into large basins of water, so that the sun's heat would extract a fine film of oil, which could then be absorbed into cotton and stored in jars.

Margaret, Duchess of Portland

1715–1785

Margaret Cavendish Bentinck, Duchess of Portland after her marriage to William Bentinck, 2nd Duke of Portland, is one of only three women to have had an entire family of roses named after them. The others are Lady Banks (*Rosa banksiae*), wife of the botanist Sir Joseph Banks, and Helen Wilson (*Rosa helenae*; see pp.156–9), whose husband was the plant hunter Ernest Wilson.

The only child of Edward Harley, 2nd Earl of Oxford, and Lady Henrietta Cavendish Holles, daughter of the Duke of Newcastle, Margaret grew up with a passion for everything. Quoted in "Duchess of Curiosities", Rebecca Stott's essay about Margaret, the Duchess's companion Mrs Delany wrote how she delighted in collecting: "Fossils and butterflys without end ... extraordinary vegetable animals of the polipus kind ... a charming horned owl ... a green worm something like a centipede."

As the daughter of an aristocrat and heiress to the Duke of Newcastle's land and fortune, Peggy, as she was known, had a charmed and privileged life, associating with nobility and politicians, poets and writers, including the satirist Alexander Pope and the writer Jonathan Swift, author of *Gulliver's Travels*. At five years of age, she was immortalised in a poem by Matthew Prior as "My noble, lovely, little Peggy". Born early in the reign of the British King George I, her life spanned the Georgian era of neoclassical architecture and the American War of Independence (1775–1783). She was a friend of King George III and Queen Charlotte.

Growing up at the family home of Wimpole Hall in Cambridgeshire, she delighted in the study of flowers and animals, an interest encouraged by both her father and her grandfather, and taught herself from the extensive family library. Many aristocratic women of that period were collectors – of flora and fauna as well as arts and antiquities – but her depth of interest in the science and philosophy of botany and biology was exceptional.

Margaret married her "Sweet Will" in 1734, at the age of nineteen, and moved to Bulstrode Hall in Buckinghamshire, part of the Portland estate. There she sponsored plant-hunting expeditions and was a patron of botanical artists. She counted many scientists, intellectuals and philosophers from around the world among her friends, encouraging, funding and

An eighteenth-century Portrait of Margaret Cavendish Bentinck, 2nd Duchess of Portland by Michael Dahl (1656–1743).

entertaining them. She acquired shells brought back by the British explorer James Cook from his voyages to the southern oceans.

The Duchess devoted her considerable talents to developing the house and garden at Bulstrode, where she lived for fifty years. She added an ancient garden, North American flowers, kitchen gardens, a shrubbery, a parterre and a menagerie with tropical birds and buffalo. She developed a collection to rival any museum of the time, with more than four thousand items – starfish and Japanese porcelain, coins and butterflies, paintings and shells. Bulstrode was known as "The Hive" because of all the activity of collecting, arranging and documenting that went on there.

However, Margaret's collection, known as "The Portland Museum", was more than an arrangement of curiosities; it was, nearly one hundred years before Charles Darwin's *On the Origin of Species*, an attempt to classify the natural world, examining and describing every species of every plant and animal that she could bring to rural Buckinghamshire.

In her extensive and beautiful gardens and park, she grew an example of every British plant. A visitor quotes: "Its millions of charms in the midst of haymaking, botanising and roses." She donated many of these rare plants, both British and foreign, to the Royal Botanic Gardens at Kew.

Margaret was married for twenty-seven years and had five children who survived to adulthood; her son William, the 3rd Duke of Portland, was twice British Prime Minister. She was widowed in 1762, after which she came into conflict with William over the running of the estates, and he eventually eliminated all her formal gardens. When asked to refashion them, the British landscape gardener Humphry Repton described her gardens as models of their kind. Fortunately, his descriptions and plans survive, providing inspiration for garden designers, scholars and botanists.

Sadly, we can no longer view her Portland Museum in its entirety. At the Duchess's London apartment in Whitehall, from 24 April 1786, some months after her death, it was sold off, piece by piece. This was by Margaret's own request: her children had not inherited her love of collecting, and thinking of their expenses, especially the funding of William's political career, she asked that the money raised be split between them.

Margaret was a remarkable woman. She was not only a keen naturalist, geologist and collector, but is reputed to have been skilled at turning wood, jet, ivory and amber. The name of the Duchess of Portland is immortalised not only by her rose, but also by a moth, a plant genus and a Roman glass vessel known as the Portland Vase, now held in the British Museum.

The rose 'Duchess of Portland'

Type of rose: Portland
Introduced: Pre-1790; officially released 1807
Breeder: Found as a seedling in Italy; released by Dupont, Malmaison, France
Other names: The Portland Rose

There is wide debate over the origins of Portland roses and how the first of this family, Rosa 'Duchess of Portland', came to be named after Margaret Bentinck. It is said to be a cross between two ancient

families, Rosa x damascena bifera ('Quatre Saisons'), the autumn Damask, and Rosa gallica Officinalis, although other authorities dispute this and attribute it to Rosa x damascena bifera x Rosa 'Slater's Crimson China'. It is also recorded as Rosa paestana, from an origin in Italy, and alternatively as Rosa 'Scarlet Four Seasons'.

Rosa 'Slater's Crimson China' is the reason that some roses are red. Scarlet roses were unknown prior to its discovery in China in 1792, after the country had opened its doors to the West. The blooms have prominent yellow stamens and are simply stunning when mass planted. Rosa 'Slater's Crimson China' has proved to be important historically, as one of the pollen parents of Hybrid Perpetual roses (the other parent being a Bourbon).

However the rose came to the Duchess, it eventually found its way to the Château de Malmaison, the manor and estate just outside Paris owned by Joséphine de Beauharnais, wife of Napoléon I. Here Joséphine's gardener, André Dupont, released it as 'Duchess of Portland' in Margaret's honour.

It has single to semi-double cerise-red blooms and is a great spectacle when in full flower. The blooms sit on a short bush with some repeat flowering, which caused a sensation in its day: it was a feature rarely known in rose plants, with the exception of two, 'Quatre Saisons' and 'Old Blush China'.

'Duchess of Portland' has a neat, tidy habit with compact growth to about one metre and lots of foliage, which can coarsen with age. Portland roses are something of an enigma. They are a small family, with probably fewer than twenty roses currently in cultivation, but their size makes them ideal for smaller gardens.

Maria Teresa, Princesse de Lamballe

1749–1792

A gentle, naïve young woman of aristocratic birth, half-Italian and half-German, Maria Teresa Luisa of Savoy became one of the best-known casualties of the French Revolution, and one of those treated most savagely. She was born in Turin into the House of Savoy, rulers of much of Italy and, at the age of seventeen, married Louis Alexandre de Bourbon, the Prince de Lamballe.

The Prince was heir to the Penthièvre fortune, which had come to the family from King Louis XIV, his great-grandfather. The title was not a sovereign one but a *titre de courtoisie* and related to one of the *seigneuries*, or feudal rural lands, from his father. Louis Alexandre was infamous for his debaucheries and affairs, and his father, the Duc de Penthièvre, had chosen Maria Teresa for her piety and beauty, in the hope that she might change his dissolute lifestyle. The Prince, however, died only sixteen months into their marriage, and before his father.

As a young and dignified widow, Maria Teresa went to live in the Duc de Penthièvre's household at the Hôtel de Toulouse in Paris and the Château de Rambouillet, in forests to the southwest of the city, before joining the court of Marie Antoinette.

At the age of twenty-one, Maria Teresa became the lifelong companion and valued confidante of the fifteen-year-old Dauphine of France. Marie Antoinette was the daughter of the Austrian Empress Maria Teresa and Francis I, the Habsburg Holy Roman Emperor, and married to the future King Louis XVI. When she later became Queen of France in 1774, she appointed her esteemed, trusted friend as Superintendent of the Queen's Household, the highest possible rank for a lady-in-waiting.

Maria Teresa has been described as somewhat melancholy, sweetly soulful, with her compassion earning her the nickname "the good angel", but it seems she was neither amusing nor clever enough for many in the French court. She was, however, devoted to her Queen, even if she was undiplomatic at times, interfering with the running of the household and omitting to send out important invitations because she felt it was beneath her. The Princesse de Lamballe's close friendship with Marie Antoinette provoked gossip and suggestions of a lesbian relationship, but love and

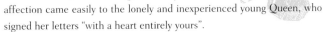

affection came easily to the lonely and inexperienced young Queen, who signed her letters "with a heart entirely yours".

Maria Teresa was an integral part of royal life, diligent and dedicated. She attended all official engagements, and it was to Maria Teresa that Marie Antoinette confessed, in the early days of her marriage, that the King had yet to make her his queen.

Replaced in the Queen's affections for some years by the Comtesse de Polignac, after 1785 Maria Teresa again became her close friend. She remained faithful even when Marie Antoinette was denounced by the French public, and the storming of the Bastille prison marked the beginning of the French Revolution and the overthrow of the King and Queen.

By October 1789, the "Declaration of the Rights of Man and of the Citizen" had effectively made France a constitutional monarchy but, with bread shortages in Paris, the situation was still worsening. Parisian women marched on Versailles and took the royal family to the Tuileries palace in the capital, where they were put under surveillance. Maria Teresa accompanied her queen into house arrest.

The only time she was not at the Queen's side was in 1791, after the royal family's abortive attempt to escape from France. Maria Teresa fled to Brussels, on her way to gain support in England, and then to the Belgian town of Spa. Meanwhile, the King and Queen, and their children, were captured at Varennes-en-Argonne, in the north-eastern region of Lorraine, and taken back to the Tuileries.

The Queen initially resisted suggestions by Antoine Barnave, a moderate deputy in the National Assembly, to persuade the Princesse to return, writing to her: "Don't come back my dear heart, don't throw yourself in the mouth of the tiger." Barnave wanted a constitutional monarchy in France, and painted a picture of a liberal régime with Marie Antoinette once again in public favour, encouraging her to call on the *émigrés*, the nobles who had fled abroad, to return. Marie Antoinette sealed her friend's fate when she succumbed at last and asked Maria Teresa to come back to her side as Superintendent. The Princesse de Lamballe spent the remainder of her short life in the service of her queen.

In the centre of this portrait (1768) by Jean Baptiste Charpentier (1728–1806), Maria Teresa holds a cup of chocolate surrounded by other members of the Penthièvre family, including her husband, who sits behind and to her right.

In September 1791, Louis XVI formally agreed to the Constitution, but then in July 1792 the extreme republican Maximilien Robespierre called for the King's removal, and in August the townspeople of Paris marched on the Tuileries. Marie Antoinette persuaded the guards to allow the Princesse to accompany them as they sought the safety of the Legislative Assembly building. During the household's discussion on what they should do, the Princesse grimly predicted: "We shall never return here."

The Assembly stripped Louis of his kingship and debated the royal family's future. On the morning of Monday 13 August, the party of thirteen prisoners, including Maria Teresa, was imprisoned in the towering medieval fortress of the Temple, where they would spend their final days.

On 19 August, the ever-sensitive and gentle Maria Teresa was taken to La Force prison, and later brought before a revolutionary tribunal to answer trumped-up charges, including performing lesbian acts, which she refuted. She was also asked to swear two oaths: one of loyalty to Liberty and Equality, and another of hatred of the King, Queen and monarchy. She agreed to the first but refused the second.

Maria Teresa was apparently firm in her resolve and, with composure, said: "I have nothing to reply, dying a little earlier or a little later is a matter of indifference to me. I am prepared to make a sacrifice of my life."

She was condemned to death, but in the prison courtyard a more ignominious fate awaited her. According to the testimony of a woman who worked there, she was felled with hammer blows to the head, hacked to death, then stripped and subjected to gross indignities. Reports from the time give differing accounts, depending in part on whether they come from the royalist or the revolutionary camp. An apprentice wax modeller, Marie Grosholz, was asked to make her death mask; the apprentice would later be known as Madame Tussaud.

Mounted on a pike, the Princesse de Lamballe's severed head, with its blonde curls, was paraded through the streets beneath Marie Antoinette's window, to jeers from the crowd demanding the Queen give her friend a final kiss. Marie Antoinette, it is reported, fainted, saving herself from the grisly sight. She thought herself responsible for her friend's death.

Louis XVI himself gave the Princesse de Lamballe a telling epitaph when he said that: "Her conduct in the course of our misfortunes amply justified the Queen's original choice of her as a friend."

The rose 'Souvenir de la Princesse de Lamballe'

Type of rose: Bourbon
Introduced: 1834
Breeder: Bréon-Mauget, France
Parentage: Unknown
Other names: Rosa 'Bourbon Queen',
Rosa 'Queen of Bourbons', Rosa 'Reine des Iles Bourbon'

This sweet little beauty, most often known by the name of 'Bourbon Queen', carries semi-double blooms of crinkled pink, loosely formed and cupped. The rose pink of the blooms is enhanced by darker magenta veining, which pales towards the petal edges. The blooms have an appearance of delicate fragility but are spectacular when the bush is in full flower during the summer. Her one fault is that she has little autumn re-bloom, but she is highly fragrant and therefore deserves a place in the garden.

This rose has copious handsome mid-green foliage, which is distinctively toothed. It is a robust, sturdy plant with thick branches growing to a metre and a half by a metre and a half and can be used as a small climber.

The charming Bourbon family of roses arose out of the first recorded hybridising between the newly found China roses and the old European families. The first plant was a chance seedling discovered in 1817 on what was then called the Ile Bourbon (now Réunion), in the Indian Ocean. Found growing close to its pollen parents, the China rose 'Old Blush' and Rosa x damascena ('Quatre Saisons'), the seedling was named 'Rose Edouard' and heralded the start of a list of fabulous roses that shared the lushness of the blooms from the old families and the silky texture and repeat-flowering gene of the new China roses. The Bourbons are excellent garden plants, which will rise to any occasion and fulfil any role asked of them.

Empress Joséphine

1763–1814

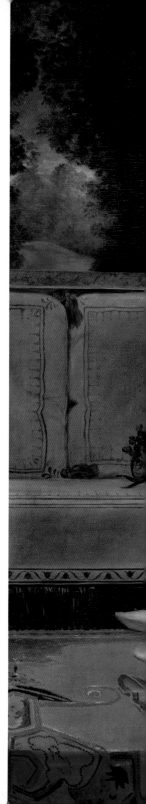

"I awake filled with you. Your image, and the intoxicating pleasures of last night, allow my senses no rest ... Amazing indeed, sweet and incomparable Joséphine, is the effect that you have wrought within my heart."

So wrote Napoléon Bonaparte to Joséphine de Beauharnais in one of his countless love letters to her, many of which survive to this day. As the first Empress of the French, Joséphine had a vital role in European history; for lovers of roses and gardens she is also an important figure, through her development of the estate at the Château de Malmaison.

Born Marie-Joseph-Rose Tascher de la Pagerie at her parents' sugar plantation on the French Caribbean island of Martinique, Joséphine was, during her early life, known as Rose; it was Napoléon who would later call her Joséphine. In 1779, with her family's financial affairs in disarray, the sixteen-year-old Joséphine set sail with her father for France. Her aunt had arranged a marriage with Alexandre de Beauharnais, later a politician and general in the Revolutionary regime.

Joséphine and Alexandre first set eyes on each other at the Breton port of Brest and were married two months later, in December 1779. They had two children: a daughter, Hortense, and a son, Eugène, before separating acrimoniously in 1785, amid accusations of infidelity on both sides. But while Alexandre certainly had mistresses, his charges against Joséphine did not stand up to investigation, and she was granted custody of the children and a generous allowance.

Before the French Revolution of 1789, Joséphine spent time in Paris, learning its manners and fashions, and two years back on Martinique. As an aristocrat, she was at some risk during the Revolution and, although she had legally separated from her husband some nine years before, Joséphine was arrested a month after him, in April 1794. They were reunited in the Carmes prison in Paris, condemned as enemies of the Revolution during the violent political repression of the Reign of Terror (September 1793 to July 1794). Alexandre was sent to the guillotine in the mass executions of the time, but Joséphine was saved when Maximilien Robespierre, the leader of the revolutionary government, was himself put to death in the

Empress Joséphine painted at Château de Malmaison (c.1801) by Baron François Pascal Simon Gérard (1770–1837).

counter-rebellion that ended the bloodshed. In 1795, a new French law meant that Joséphine could reclaim Alexandre's fortune.

Joséphine had several affairs with rich and powerful men, who helped her as she sought to find a place in society. Her daughter Hortense recorded in her diaries her mother saying: "My child, you must remember since your father's death, I have done nothing but try to save the remains of his fortune that we feared would be lost. Must I not be grateful to those who have helped and protected me?"

She met Général Napoléon Bonaparte in 1795, when he was a rising star of the republican army, having extinguished the royalist rebellion in Paris in the battle of 13 Vendémiaire (the revolutionary calendar's rendition of 5 October 1795). She became his mistress, and they married the following year, when she was thirty-three and he was twenty-seven.

Their relationship has become immortalised as one of the great and enduring love affairs of history. It would seem that Joséphine was the perfect foil for the irascible, ambitious Napoléon, with her rather sweet, docile demeanour. It has been reported that she was never anything other than perfectly groomed and elegant, whether she was at a state function or in the garden at Malmaison, the estate she bought for herself and Napoléon while he was on his Egyptian campaign in 1799.

She was an inveterate spendthrift, borrowing money and selling her own jewellery to purchase Malmaison, but she was also charming, lively and devoted to her family. Both had relationships outside the marriage, but Napoléon was so enamoured of Joséphine that he forgave her extravagance, tolerated her lack of correspondence, despaired at her infidelities and enjoyed the comforts she provided.

Joséphine was profligate with her husband's money; it was her vision and energy and his funds that led to the development of Malmaison as a repository for every known rose. When she acquired the estate, just west of Paris, it was a ramshackle, rundown manor house with one hundred and fifty acres of woodland and meadows. She hired architects to redecorate in what became the Empire style, with its influences from ancient Rome. Her gardens followed the English fashion, with sweeps of lawn and open vistas framed by trees. She was the first in France to grow tree peonies, camellias and purple magnolias, and she nurtured her tender plants in a heated greenhouse.

In November 1799 her husband led a coup that overthrew the established government and made himself First Consul; in 1804, after several plots against him, Napoléon crowned himself Emperor of France at the cathedral of Nôtre Dame in Paris and placed the crown of an empress on Joséphine's head.

Their marriage was characterised by his frequent absences at war, which brought Joséphine fear and despair. When he set off to Spain during the Peninsular War, Hortense wrote in her diary: "The Empress was even sadder than ever to see the Emperor go. 'Will you ever cease your warmongering?' she asked him."

Increasingly, pressure mounted on Joséphine to produce an heir, which became essential to the survival of the marriage. When she failed to do so, Napoléon's family pushed him to divorce her. Reluctantly, with great sorrow, he did so on 15 December 1809, and in the spring of the following year he married Marie Louise of Austria, who bore him a son. In her acceptance of the inevitability of divorce, Joséphine wrote: "Yet God is my witness that I love him more than my life, and much more than that throne, that crown which he has given me."

The distraught Joséphine retired to Malmaison, where she continued to acquire roses. She grew around four hundred varieties, the majority of them Gallicas, aiming to cultivate an example of every rose in existence. Many of her plant specimens can be seen in intricate engravings, immortalised by the celebrated botanical illustrator Pierre-Joseph Redouté, who had taken on the grandiose project of portraying and describing the flower species in the gardens. "Les Roses" was the last work that Joséphine commissioned from him, although she did not live to see its completion.

Joséphine died suddenly, from a "malignant and putrid disease" thought to have been diphtheria. Her son, when informing Napoléon of her death, wrote: "She died with the courage, serenity and resignation of an angel."

Today, the Musée National du Château de Malmaison, Joséphine's home, has been restored to much of its former glory, and the gardens are also being renovated to regain their grandeur and stand as a fitting memorial to this extraordinary woman.

The rose 'Empress Joséphine'

Type of rose: Gallica (*Rosa gallica* x *Rosa pendulina,* but also described as
Rosa gallica x *cinnamonea*)
Introduced: Unknown; named around 1814
Breeder: Unknown; introduced by Dupont, Malmaison, France
Parentage: Described as a sport of *Rosa majalis* (also known as the Cinnamon Rose)

That a Gallica rose is named after Joséphine is fitting tribute to a Frenchwoman who did more than anyone else to cherish, collect and protect old roses, and in particular her native Rosa gallica. Her enthusiasm and extravagance have ensured that early varieties of rose, and the varieties that evolved from them, survive for our enjoyment today.

The plant grown today as 'Empress Joséphine' is most probably Rosa francofurtana, a rose discovered either by John Tradescant the elder in 1618 in Russia, or by Charles de l'Ecluse in 1583. No one is quite sure. It is said to have been Joséphine's favourite, growing wild in the hedges. It is a beautiful rose, worthy of its new title, and was probably named after Joséphine sometime after her death, as no rose by that name was listed in her collection at Malmaison.

That collection was achieved thanks to her niece, Stéphanie Tascher, and the noted horticulturalist, rosarian and nurseryman, Louis Parmentier, who administered Stéphanie's estate in Belgium. They gained a special licence to bring plants to France for Joséphine during the naval blockade by Britain in the Napoleonic Wars.

'Empress Joséphine' is a tall shrub, growing to a metre and a half in height, with wonderful arching canes. The large blooms are tissue-like in texture and translucent, ragged and loosely double with a light fragrance. The petals are deep pink, with darker veining, and flushed with lavender and purple. It is elegantly dressed, with tough grey-green leaves corrugated by deep veins, and is relatively thornless.

André Dupont, who introduced this rose, came under Joséphine's protection as the first grower and collector of roses in France. He had his own beautiful collection of more than one hundred and ten species or varieties of rose, and they collaborated to develop Malmaison. Dupont, also recognised by a rose, was the founder and director of the collection at the Jardin du Luxembourg in Paris.

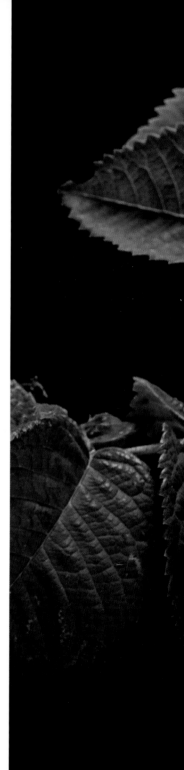

Aimée Dubucq de Rivéry

c.1763–1817

"You will be sent to Europe to complete your schooling. Your ship will be seized by corsairs. You will be taken and placed in a *seraglio*. There you will give birth to a son. Your son will reign gloriously but the steps to the throne will be dyed with the blood of his predecessor. As to you, you will never taste the outward honours of the court, but you will live in a great and splendid palace where you will reign supreme. At the very hour when you know your happiness is won, that happiness will fade like a dream, and a lingering illness will carry you to your tomb."

These words, reportedly spoken by an old seer to the young Aimée Dubucq de Rivéry and recounted in *The Wilder Shores of Love* by Lesley Blanch, begin the astounding story of a woman shrouded in mystery, and whose rose is the exotically named 'La Belle Sultane'.

Aimée was born on the French-Caribbean island of Martinique, where her father owned a plantation, and was a cousin of the future Empress Joséphine of France. It was an intimate friend of Joséphine – Mademoiselle Lenormand, a well-known Parisian clairvoyant – who first recounted the story of the visit made by the two young girls to the old seer who lived near Joséphine's family home on the Caribbean island. Joséphine was given the prophecy that one day she would become "more than a queen", while the extraordinary predictions for Aimée were to define her future story.

At the age of about thirteen, Aimée was sent to a convent school at Nantes in France. On a return voyage to Martinique, her ship sought refuge from a fierce storm in the Mediterranean. It disappeared, possibly attacked by Barbary corsairs, pirates from the Barbary Coast of North Africa.

From here on, Aimée's story is impossible to prove, but it has inspired biographers and novelists through the centuries. According to the tale, the pirates took the ship and seized the beautiful girl they found on board. Recognising their prize, they treated Aimée well, before eventually sending her as a gift to the Ottoman Sultan Abdulhamid I, whose harem she entered at the Topkapi Palace in Istanbul.

The Ottoman Empire was vast and included lands now forming Greece, and parts of Iraq, Egypt, Libya, Bulgaria, Romania and the Balkan states. It was not unusual for women of different cultures therefore to enter the

A detail from the nineteenth-century painting entitled *Dreams* by Edouard Frederic Wilhelm Richter (1844–1913).

Ottoman *seraglio*, or palace, and there to be given a Turkish name that reflected their particular qualities. The Sultan was delighted with his gift of Aimée and renamed her Naksh, "The Beautiful One".

Prized for her fair skin and golden hair, Naksh became the sultan's fourth wife. According to the stories of her life as Naksh, Aimée possessed tremendous spirit, which helped her to survive the traumas and politics of her new environment. The mother of the future Mahmud II, she became embroiled in harem machinations as the sultan's wives fought and conspired for their own sons to become Abdulhamid's heir.

After the old Sultan's death in 1789, his nephew and successor, Selim III, introduced Turkey to new ideas. Aimée is said to have become Selim's advisor and confidante, teaching him French, encouraging him to appoint the first French ambassador in 1797, and bringing French artists and architects to the court.

Through the late eighteenth century and during the course of the Napoleonic Wars, the Ottoman Empire was exposed to attacks from Russia, Great Britain and France, and would make alliances with one while being at war with another. The reforming Selim promoted a closer relationship with France and wanted to remodel the Ottoman army along western lines. He believed that Napoléon Bonaparte, by then married to Aimée's cousin Joséphine, would help in his progressive enterprise, but Napoléon had other ideas. He took command of the French army in Egypt and, in 1799, marched on the Ottoman province of Damascus in Syria.

In Istanbul, harem politics and motherly ambitions never rested. In 1807, Selim was deposed and imprisoned after his army rebelled against his Francophile reforms. It is thought that Aisha Sina Pervar, another consort of Sultan Abdulhamid, was the power behind the cause of her stepson Mustapha, son of the Sultan's first wife. Mustapha IV was made sultan, and Selim was assassinated. Aimée and her son Mahmud, who was next in line to the throne, were also in danger. Mahmud hid in the palace, and only narrowly escaped being murdered.

Mustapha's brief reign was marked by brutality and the slaughter of anyone suspected of supporting Selim. But Mahmud's allies prevailed, overthrowing Mustapha and eventually fulfilling the prophesy given to Aimée by the seer on Martinique. In 1808, he became Sultan Mahmud II and embarked on significant reforms, which have been attributed largely to his mother's influence. After two decades behind the walls of the harem of Topkapi, Aimée became the Sultan Valide, the "Mother of the Sultan". She was, at last, "La Belle Sultane".

When she died nine years later, in 1817, Aimée is said to have received the last sacraments from a French monk in Istanbul; possibly the only time a Catholic priest has ever entered a harem.

Some historians have questioned whether Aimée and Naksh really were the same person, pointing out discrepancies in dates, and arguing that Aimée could not be Mahmud's mother as, at the time of his birth in 1785, she is documented as being a witness to a wedding in France. But equally other biographies contain much convincing evidence to support the story.

Mahmud, overwhelmed with grief, buried his mother in the gardens of the Fatih Mosque in Istanbul. He composed the epitaph on her grave, and celebrated her with the words:

"Her highness and fame made of a country a rose garden."

The rose 'La Belle Sultane'

Type of rose: Gallica
Introduced: Probably a "found" rose from
the Netherlands in the eighteenth century
Breeder: Unknown; introduced by Dupont,
Malmaison, France
Other names: *Rosa gallica Violacea*,
Rosa 'Maheka'

*'La Belle Sultane' is a stunning rose,
as evocative as her name, and stands tall
and proud in our garden. There is no
hint of the subdued concubine about
her, as she does not hide her beauty.
Her flowers are slightly more than single,
a sumptuous velvety crimson-purple,
the traditional colour of the Gallicas,
with a halo of deep golden stamens at the
centre. The blooms turn to a soft purple
with brownish tinges as they age.*

*She flowers freely on an upright shrub,
with sparse foliage on prickly canes. Her
head nods imperiously above lesser roses,
and her colour, with the contrasting
golden stamens, jolts the eye to startled
surprise. She spreads her favours
throughout the garden, colonising
wherever she goes, as she suckers readily
if grown on her own roots.*

*The rose was acquired by André
Dupont for the grounds of the Château
de Malmaison, and is recorded by the
gardener Jules Gravereaux in his list
of Joséphine's roses. Dupont, as the first
nurseryman to practise hand pollination,
was considered to be the premier French
rose breeder. It has been said of him that:
"He is an enchanter who submits the rose
to his magic wand and forces it to
undergo the most surprising and
agreeable transformation."*

*Dupont was a director of the Jardin du
Luxembourg in Paris and then gardener
at Malmaison for Joséphine, wife of
Napoléon Bonaparte. It seems likely that
the relationship between Joséphine and
Aimée, and the story that eventually
unfolded, influenced his decision to
name this rose after his patron's cousin.*

Marie de Sombreuil

1768–1823

The sumptuous rose known as 'Mme de Sombreuil' is our very favourite. It was named after Jeanne Jacques Marie Anne Françoise de Virot, who was known as Marie-Maurille Virot de Sombreuil, a beautiful young aristocrat who saved her father from the September Massacres of 1792, during the terrors that followed the French Revolution.

Marie's father, the old Charles François de Virot, Marquis de Sombreuil, was a royalist commander who had been made governor of the veterans' home of Les Invalides and its armoury. As revolutionaries marched on the domed buildings of Les Invalides on the morning of 14 July 1789, the Marquis tried to disable the rifles in his charge. In spite of the insubordination of his troops, he refused to deliver arms to the new militia. The mob broke in and seized around thirty thousand rifles, but without any gunpowder or shot. The revolutionary crowd stormed the La Bastille prison to secure this ammunition, and more weapons, in one of the defining events of the 1789 revolution.

The events for which Marie became known and immortalised as the "Heroine of the Glass of Blood" took place a few years later in 1792 when her father was arrested and imprisoned. He was suspected of assisting the royal family and of anti-revolutionary activism and was held with other aristocrats at the l'Abbaye prison in Saint-Germain-des-Prés, where conditions were so cramped the prisoners could not even sit down. Marie was imprisoned at the same time as her father but was separated from him and, together with two other young women also there to support male relatives, she was made to spend the nights in the gaoler's room.

With Prussian forces invading eastern France, Paris was in a state of hysteria. On 2 September, the massacres began as the mob killed and mutilated the inmates of the city's revolutionary prisons. Despite being told by the guards that they would be safe, two of the women at l'Abbaye were butchered as they tried to leave.

Marie made her way through the mob to her father and appeared with him before a makeshift tribunal. She pleaded with the court that her father was an old man, and that they should take pity on him, and declared that they could strike him only through her.

This 1853 painting by Pierre Puvis de Chavannes (1824–1898) shows Marie de Sombreuil as she reaches for a glass of blood, which she must drink to save her father's life.

Impressed by this passionate outburst, the master of the guillotine demanded that Marie prove her intent by drinking a cupful of fresh aristocratic blood. He handed her a glass from the bloody platform. She did not hesitate or shudder. She drank, and, with the applause of the crowd ringing in her ears, went with her father to safety. It was generally believed that the glass held blood, although Marie de Sombreuil herself is said to have insisted that it was only red wine.

Safety in those times was short lived, and Marie earned her father only a brief reprieve. In 1793, the Marquis was again imprisoned, and Marie again followed him. When they returned to l'Abbaye, accounts describe how all the inmates rose in her honour. Marie's father and the older of her two brothers, Stanislas, were accused of conspiring to help imprisoned aristocrats escape, and were guillotined in 1794. Marie survived and has been hailed as a great heroine and model of filial virtue.

In 1796, she married the Comte de Villelume, but little is known of her life after this. She is recorded as having petitioned the Restoration King, Louis XVIII, for a pension to educate her son, as her later years were passed in reduced circumstances. But the legend of Marie is recalled in the painting by Puvis de Chavannes, in the name of one of the most beautiful of roses, and in a poem by Victor Hugo:

*"Et Sombreuil, qui trahit par ses pâleurs soudaines
Ce sang glacé des morts circulant dans ses veines."*

"And Sombreuil, who betrays her sudden palour
With the ice-cold blood of the dead in her veins."

The rose 'Mme de Sombreuil'

Type of rose: Climbing Tea
Introduced: 1850
Breeder: Robert, Angers, France
Parentage: Unknown (Stephen Scanniello), or possibly *Gigantesque* x unknown Hybrid Perpetual (Graham Stuart Thomas)

There are discrepancies in descriptions and photos of this rose. Some accounts describe a cream, loosely petalled rose, while others write of her as heavily fragrant with tight petals. Scanniello states that the flower we know as 'Mme de Sombreuil' is not the one recorded in nineteenth-century literature. This is confirmed by Peter Harkness in "The Rose: An Illustrated History". However, rosarians Peter Beales, Roger Phillips and Martin Rix, and other notables in the rose world, describe Sombreuil differently from Scannellio and Harkness.

Whatever the true provenance of this rose, the plant we grow in our garden as 'Mme de Sombreuil' is a rose to be treasured and we would never be without it. Her blooms are of a heavy cream with tinges of flesh pink in the buds and at the centres of the fully opened flowers. They are flat and quartered and wonderfully fragrant, with a delicious tea scent.

This rose will grow as a bush and as a small climber, and in our climate is never without a bloom. It is a slightly inelegant shrub clothed with ample, lush green foliage. 'Mme de Sombreuil' has the reputation of being slightly frost tender, but here in New Zealand, she survives untroubled by frosts – or revolution. As "The Graham Stuart Thomas Rose Book" says, she is to be "treasured for all time".

Adélaïde d'Orléans

1777–1847

Adélaïde d'Orléans was a member of the ruling French Bourbon family, and the much-loved sister of Louis-Philippe, the last King of France. She was embroiled in the French Revolution and the turmoil of the Napoleonic era, so her life was characterised by instability and exile, but also by a staunch loyalty to her family.

Her parents were Louis-Philippe-Joseph and Louise-Marie of Bourbon, the flamboyant Duc and Duchesse d'Orléans, two of the wealthiest nobles in France. They were alienated from the court of Louis XVI and Marie Antoinette and, when the revolution came in 1789, the Duc d'Orléans's liberal sympathies led him to side with the revolutionaries against the royal family. He became known as Philippe Egalité, and at Louis XVI's trial he voted for the King's execution.

Adélaïde's parents became estranged and she did not see her mother until she was sixteen. Adélaïde and her brother were brought up and educated by her father's mistress, Madame de Genlis, a cultured woman who also supported the ideals of the revolution. Madame de Genlis was an integral part of the royal household.

After Louis XVI's execution in January 1793, and during the Reign of Terror that began in September that year, aristocrats fled France in fear. Adélaïde's brother, Louis-Philippe, urged Madame de Genlis to take his sister out of the country. They escaped and met up with Louis-Philippe in Switzerland; shortly thereafter, arrest warrants were issued for all members of the Bourbon family. Despite his support of the people, Adélaïde's father was condemned by a revolutionary court and sent to the guillotine.

Adélaïde lived in exile for twenty-one years, moving between several European countries before settling with her brother in England, following his return from several years in the Americas. In 1814, the monarchy was reinstated and Adélaïde went back with Louis-Philippe to France. She became his closest friend, confidante and counsellor; the remaining members of the family were hardly ever separated. She was privately married to one of his *aides de camp*, Général Baron Athalin, a former officer in Napoléon's army and a respected scientist and engineer.

A nineteenth-century portrait of Adélaïde, Duchesse d'Orléans, by Marie-Amélie Cogniet (1798–1869).

87

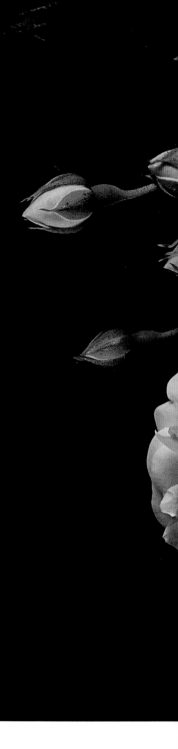

In 1830, Adélaïde saw Louis-Philippe crowned the "Citizen King" of France, a self-styled king of the people, after the reactionary Charles X was forced to abdicate. Following the July Revolution, the elected Chamber of Deputies had called for the liberal Louis-Philippe to take the throne. Adélaïde responded: "If you believe that the adherence of our family can be useful to the Revolution, we will give it to you willingly."

"Madame Adélaïde" was intelligent and witty: Louis-Philippe frequently sought her opinion on matters of state and she often acted as his regent. According to her obituary, she was: "A woman of firm judgement and of the calmest and most reflective courage."

Adélaïde died in December 1847, following a long illness. Two months later her brother abdicated in the face of increasing unrest. Distraught at his sister's death, Louis-Philippe fell into a deep depression. Her niece noted: "To him the loss is irretrievable. My aunt lived but for him, one may almost say that her affections alone had kept her alive these last years."

The rose 'Adélaïde d'Orléans'

Type of rose: Hybrid Sempervirens
Introduced: 1826
Breeder: Jacques, Orléans, France
Parentage: *Rosa sempervirens x Rosa* 'Parson's Pink China'
Other names: *Rosa* 'Léopoldine d'Orléans'

This once-flowering rose is a herald of spring. The first rose of the year to bloom in our garden in New Zealand (although it may be later in northern Europe), it has exquisite flowers that are worth the ten-month wait and a beautiful weeping form, with blooms that hang in clusters. The buds are a deep rose pink and open to creamy-white flowers with a hint of blush at their centres.

The Victorians knew the Sempervirens family as the "evergreen rose", and 'Adélaïde d'Orléans' has lush, shiny, evergreen foliage. It is a vigorous yet discreet rambler with tiny, grasping prickles on long, flexible canes. Its musk scent is shared by all Sempervirens roses.

Antoine A. Jacques (1782–1866), head gardener to Adélaïde's brother, Louis-Philippe, was mainly responsible for this tiny family of Hybrid Sempervirens roses, which used Rosa sempervirens as the pollen parent. The son of a gardener, Jacques became a respected horticulturalist, writer and administrator of the Orléans family estates. However, when Louis-Philippe abdicated, Jacques was also forced to flee, and the last years of his life were spent in impoverished circumstances, despite his long and distinguished career.

His roses, however, have proved a lasting testament to his skill as a rose grower: in 1819, he sowed the first seed of 'Rose Edouard', the natural crossing between Rosa x damascena bifera ('Quatre Saisons') and the China rose 'Old Blush' from the Ile Bourbon, which formed the basis of the Bourbon rose family. This line lives on today through the beautiful 'Souvenir de la Malmaison', 'Souvenir de la Princesse Lamballe' (see p.69; most often known as 'Bourbon Queen') and others.

Marie Thérèse, Duchesse d'Angoulême

1778–1851

Marie Antoinette, Queen of France, greeted the birth of her first child with the words: "Poor little girl. You are not what was desired but you are no less dear to me on that account. A son would have been the property of the state. You shall be mine."

Marie Thérèse Charlotte of France, later Duchesse d'Angoulême, was the eldest daughter of Marie Antoinette and Louis XVI. In a life of turmoil, imprisonment and exile, she would become the sole survivor of her family and, for the briefest of moments, Queen of France herself.

As the eldest daughter of the King, Marie Thérèse was known as "Madame Royale" and, for the first ten years of her life, she enjoyed all the luxuries of the extravagant court. Then, in 1789, the revolution erupted in Paris. Women revolutionaries marched on the royal residence at Versailles, to protest at the high cost of bread, and stormed the building. After a night-long stand-off, the royal family was forced to return with them to the Tuileries Palace and put under house arrest.

At first, life was relatively normal, and the family retained many of its royal privileges. But, as the political situation worsened, two years later the King and Queen, with their twelve-year-old daughter and her youngest brother Louis Charles (another brother had died in 1789), made a desperate attempt to flee to safety. However, they were recognised and captured at Varennes-en-Argonne, only a few miles from the German border.

With calls for a republic growing fiercer, in 1792 the family was incarcerated in the notorious Temple prison and the rule of Louis XVI was suspended. In January 1793, Louis was guillotined; several months later Marie Antoinette was taken to the squalid Conciergerie prison – and her children were never to see her again. As they parted, Marie Antoinette tenderly embraced her daughter and told her to have courage. The Queen was then questioned over three days and nights, during which time the judges were alarmed by her obvious dignity and feared it would inspire others. Dignity alone, however, could not save her and she was executed in October as mobs in the streets howled for her death.

Marie Thérèse learned only much later of the fate of her family. She subsequently wrote of her mother: "She went to her death with courage,

This portrait (1784) by Elisabeth Louise Vigée-Lebrun (1755–1842) shows a young Marie Thérèse with her first brother, the Dauphin Louis-Joseph-Xavier, who died when he was eight years old.

amid curses which the unhappy, misguided people poured forth against her. Her courage did not abandon her in the cart, nor on the scaffold; she showed as much in death as she had shown in life."

Young Marie Thérèse made repeated attempts to see her brother, now claimed by the royalists as King Louis XVII. She was unaware that he was confined alone in a filthy cell where, at the age of ten, he died of sickness and starvation. For the rest of her life, she was haunted by stories that he had been saved, but of all those who came forward claiming to be the lost Dauphin, none was ever found to be genuine.

Miraculously, Marie Thérèse survived imprisonment and the Reign of Terror, becoming known as "The Orphan of the Temple". Scratched on the wall of her room were the words: "Marie Thérèse is the most unhappy creature in the world. She can obtain no news of her mother; nor be united to her, though she has asked it a thousand times. Live my good Mother! Whom I love well, but of whom I can bear no tidings. O my Father! Watch over me from the heaven above. O my God! Forgive those who have made my family die." She was finally released at the age of seventeen and went to Austria, her mother's homeland, to live within the Viennese court of her cousin, the Emperor Francis II.

Her ambitious uncle, Louis-Stanislas-Xavier, had proclaimed himself Louis XVIII upon the death of Louis-Charles and was determined to maintain the Bourbon dynasty. In 1799, he arranged for Marie Thérèse to be married to her cousin, Louis-Antoine, Duc d'Angoulême, now second in line to the French throne. From then on, her fortunes were bound to those of her husband and the royal House of Bourbon. It was another kind of prison for Marie Thérèse, as her marriage to Louis-Antoine was deeply unhappy. In his postscript to her diaries, nineteenth-century French critic Charles Augustin Sainte-Beuve asked: "Did Madame d'Angoulême ever have a single day of happiness after her issue from the Temple?"

During the rule of Napoléon Bonaparte, from the time he became First Consul in 1799, the Duc and Duchesse d'Angoulême lived in Britain, Poland and Russia. Their long years of exile came to an end in 1814, when Napoléon was defeated and the French monarchy restored. Marie Thérèse returned to France, and the next years were spent re-establishing the French court under the reigns of her two uncles, first Louis XVIII and then Charles X. When Napoléon escaped from imprisonment on the island of Elba in February 1815, Marie Thérèse attempted to organise a resistance.

It failed when the royal troops defected to join Napoléon, but, for her bravery, he afterwards described her as: "The only man of her race."

Exiled again, she returned four months later for the last time after Napoléon was recaptured and sent to St Helena, an island off the west coast of Africa. The monarchy was again restored and, when Charles X abdicated during the July Revolution of 1830, Marie Thérèse and Louis-Antoine became Queen and King of France for a mere twenty minutes, before Louis-Antoine also relinquished his claim to the crown and Louis-Philippe became the "Citizen King". The Duc and Duchesse then left France for permanent exile.

Marie Thérèse outlived both her husband and her uncle, spending her last years in Austria, sustained, as she had been throughout her life, by her fortitude and strong faith. Twenty-one years after her final departure from France, she died aged seventy-two. She was laid to rest between Charles X and her husband the Duc d'Angoulême in the chapel of the Franciscans on the Kostanjevica Hill, now on the Slovenian border with Italy.

An early nineteenth-century portrait of Marie Thérèse attributed to Friedrich Heinrich Füger (1751–1818).

The Rose
'Duchesse d'Angoulême'

Type of rose: Gallica
Introduced: c.1835
Breeder: Vibert, Angers, France
Parentage: Unknown

'Duchesse d'Angoulême' is a luscious rose with a rich, powerful fragrance. Its deep pink buds open to lovely blush-pink blooms, which are small and saucer-shaped with slightly re-curved petals. It is also called the Wax Rose, an indication of the clarity and translucence of its petals. The delicate blooms are arranged in soft clusters that nod gently in the breeze.

Although it does not have the strong royal purple colours of most Gallicas, it is typical in all other respects, with coarse, matte green leaves. A tidy, arching shrub, refined as any duchess should be, it grows to barely waist height and has almost thornless canes.

Jean-Pierre Vibert (1777–1866), the most prolific rose breeder in nineteenth-century France, specialised in Gallicas and created more than six hundred varieties, sixty of which are still grown today. With the parentage of 'Duchesse d'Angoulême' unknown, there is some debate among rosarians as to whether it is a Gallica or a Centifolia cross; Vibert himself described it as a Gallica.

Louise Antoinette, Duchesse de Montebello

1782–1856

An outstanding beauty of Napoleonic France, Louise Antoinette de Guéhéneuc was the daughter of François Scholastique, Comte de Guéhéneuc, a financer and senator. She was said to resemble paintings of the Madonna by Italian Renaissance master Raphael, with a face charmingly pale and virginal, and Napoléon Bonaparte for a time regarded her grace and demeanour as the model for all other women to imitate. She has been described variously as icily beautiful, chaste, avaricious and envious. She was also said to have been a diehard Jacobin, a supporter of the most radical movement of the French Revolution.

Louise Antoinette was not part of the nobility, belonging to the "*bonne bourgeoisie*", or professional and mercantile middle class, but her family's riches assisted her move into Parisian society. Here she came to the attention of Napoléon Bonaparte, who liked to arrange splendid marriages. He matched her with Maréchal Jean Lannes, one of his most favoured generals. Lannes records in his memoirs that he and Louise Antoinette met at a grand ball, where he danced with two women: one, a blonde who initially captivated him, and the other, a brunette whom he eventually married on 15 September 1800.

Lannes was later made Duc de Montebello, honoured after the battle near the town in Lombardy, Italy, which he had been instrumental in winning. Unlike other matches made by Napoléon, it seems he and the Duchesse had a happy marriage, but in 1809 she was left a young widow with five small children.

Lannes died from a shot wound to his knees at the Battle of Aspern-Essling, near Vienna. Desolate about the horrors of war, accounts say he sat on the edge of a ditch during a lull in fighting and his crossed legs were hit by a shell. One leg was amputated immediately without anaesthetic by the roadside and the other was removed later. But resulting infection in his wounds caused his death some days afterwards. Louise Antoinette was said to be inconsolable at his death and retired to the solace of her children.

In a letter to the Duchesse, Napoléon wrote: "My cousin the Marshall died this morning of wounds received on the field of honour. My sorrow equalises yours. The General was the most distinguished from my armies,

Louise Antoinette with her five children, painted by Baron François Pascal Simon Gérard (1770–1837).

my comrade for years, and the one I have regarded as my best friend. Your children will always have rights particular to my protection and I give assurance of that."

True to his promise, Napoléon recalled the Duchesse de Montebello to court and in recognition of Lannes's service he appointed her Dame d'Honneur, chief lady-in-waiting to his second wife, Marie Louise, the successor to the Empress Joséphine. Hortense, Joséphine's daughter by her first marriage, wrote of how the Duchesse was: "Admired by all, still young and beautiful, her appointment proved that the Emperor did not forget those heroes who had died for their country's causes."

She recovered eventually to take up her post at the side of the new Empress, exerting her influence on the affairs of state and the imperial household. She secretly hated Napoléon and disliked life at court, but became one of the few close friends of the lonely and susceptible young Empress. Hortense describes how Marie Louise had a "sort of adoration [for the Duchesse] which seemed strange to so many people."

The new Empress was a virtual prisoner in her gilded cage, kept from anyone who had not been presented to Napoléon. The Duchesse became her conduit to the world, divulging petty squabbles and enlivening her sheltered life with the latest society gossip. She was also the Empress's closest confidante, refusing Napoléon's request that she spy on her mistress.

The Duchesse de Montebello, described by Marie Louise in her letters to Napoléon as "La Duchesse", became indispensable. She was responsible for the day-to-day affairs of Marie Louise, weaving her way through court intrigues and disputes, keeping her apart from other influences. She stayed loyal to the Empress and was suspected by Napoléon of persuading her to reject his request that she join him in exile on the island of Elba. Louise Antoinette earned his withering contempt for this act of "betrayal".

After Napoléon's imprisonment and Marie Louise's flight to Austria in 1814, the Duchesse de Montebello returned to an obscure existence, apparently without regret, and lived a further forty-two years with her children and family. She refused an offer of marriage to King Ferdinand VII of Spain, preferring to honour the proud name that she bore valiantly.

A nineteenth-century miniature of
Louise Antoinette by Jean Baptiste
Isabey (1767–1855).

The rose 'Duchesse de Montebello'

Type of rose: Gallica
Introduced: 1829
Breeder: Laffay, Auteuil, France
Parentage: Unknown, possibly Gallica x China

This rose is as icily beautiful and softly refined as her namesake. Pretty as a Victorian picture, 'Duchesse de Montebello' has small, double and perfectly quartered blooms of a soft, feminine pink, paling with age to a light flesh pink. The flowers bloom early on a tidy, robust bush, the canes flowing to the ground when heavily laden. The renowned New Zealand rosarian Nancy Steen must have loved this rose because, in "The Charm of Old Roses", she describes her in such glowing terms: "The smallish flowers, which look as though they have been created artificially by placing fold upon fold of beautifully moulded and swathed blush-pink chiffon round a pale green button eye, are a sheer delight and are always admired, both on the tall bush in the garden and in old-rose arrangements."

Such a rare beauty is given free rein in our garden, where she suckers well. She will cope with a little shade, as was the wont of the genteel ladies of yesteryear, and her foliage is grey-green and plentiful. This gentle charmer, which is untypical in colour for a Gallica, cannot, in my opinion, be omitted from any garden; she is one of the select roses I have taken with me to our new home.

Jean Laffay, who introduced 'Duchesse de Montebello', was born in Paris in 1794 and began his career as a gardener to a nurseryman. He bred roses over a long period, from 1815 to 1855, and is recognised as the father of Hybrid Perpetuals. He did not hand-pollinate his roses, relying on natural fertilisation, raising some two hundred thousand seedlings annually. It seems a shame that the breeder of such a fine Gallica, through his seditious development of Hybrid Perpetuals, ensured the gradual decline of the once-flowering varieties like 'Duchesse de Montebello'.

Duchesse d'Auerstädt

Louise Aimée Julie Leclerc (1782–1868) / Jeanne Alice de Voize (c.1845–c.1936)

This rose may have been dedicated to the second wife of one of Napoléon's marshals, who even as a soldier abroad on lengthy campaigns found time to write her beautiful and touching letters. Or perhaps, more likely, it was named after the wife of the marshal's nephew, born some sixty-three years after the first Duchesse, and a society belle at the time the rose was presented. With no clear record to decide which of these women was officially commemorated by the intense, subtly golden blooms of 'Duchesse d'Auerstädt', I have included both their stories.

Napoléon Bonaparte's "Iron Marshal", Maréchal Louis Nicolas Davout, Duc d'Auerstedt (he spelt his title with an "e"), was married twice. Davout – originally spelt d'Avout but changed to its less aristrocratic form in the early years of the French Revolution – was the most able of all Napoléon's generals, and a strict disciplinarian with his troops. His second wife was Louise Aimée Julie Leclerc, sister of Général Charles Leclerc – himself married to Pauline Bonaparte, Napoléon's younger sister.

Aimée, as she was known by Davout, was a delightful eighteen-year-old when they met; the favoured daughter in a prominent wealthy family. Their marriage, a year later in 1801, drew her ambitious husband into the greater Bonaparte family.

During the first fourteen years of their marriage, Davout was away at war much of the time. He wrote in a letter to his "*petite* Aimée": "Your heart, all your rare and precious qualities are never far from my mind. Receive a thousand kisses from your Louis." Nevertheless, he soon returned to his bachelor habits.

It is recorded that Aimée gave birth to twelve infants, but only four survived into adulthood. As a devoted mother, she despaired at the loss of her children. She suffered poor health and depression, preferring to live a quiet life on their estate at Savigny-sur-Orge, to the south of Paris, away from the French court. Her husband eventually told her somewhat sharply that: "She had better take care of her health, and be more concerned with her unborn child than with the one which is dead."

In spite of his prolonged absences, Davout took an interest in his sons' education. In one letter he exhorted: "I would recommend to you that you

This nineteenth-century engraving, after a painting by Henri-Pierre Danloux (1753–1809), shows Louise Aimée Julie Leclerc, Duchesse d'Auerstedt, with two of her twelve children.

inspire in our two sons a strong hatred for the English and Russians." He repeatedly encouraged Aimée to spend more time in Paris and attend to court matters, but she remained reclusive.

With the collapse of the Empire in 1815, the family fell from favour and their fortunes diminished, both socially and financially. Davout was arrested, exiled and eventually pardoned by the new King Louis XVIII after swearing his allegiance. He died in 1823 at the age of fifty-three. Aimée outlived her husband by forty-five years, living until the year in which the typewriter was patented and the first official bicycle race was held in the Parc de Saint-Cloud in Paris.

Twenty years later, at the time the rose 'Duchesse d'Auerstädt' was introduced, our second duchess was a leading light in French society.

Jeanne Alice de Voize had married Léopold d'Avout, Aimée's nephew and heir to the d'Avout titles, in 1868. By this time the spelling of the family name had reverted back to its aristocratic origins, and Napoléon III had granted an edict reinstating the title of Duc d'Auerstaedt. With no remaining male heirs in Aimée's line, the dukedom was given to Léopold, the youngest son of the Maréchal's brother, Charles.

Léopold was also a soldier and suffered a serious accident while fighting on the side of the imperial government against the Paris Commune, the radical local authority set up following the French defeat in the Franco-Prussian War (1870–1871). In the last days of the conflict he suffered a direct hit to the head from a bullet, but survived and was promoted to Brigadier General for his valour, and posted as military governor to Lyon.

This central French city, where the Rhône and Saône rivers meet, is the link to the 'Duchesse d'Auerstädt' rose. Bred by Lyon grower Alexandre Bernaix, the rose was introduced in 1888, at a time when Jeanne Alice and Léopold were influential in Lyon society. As was normal at that time, Bernaix may well have elected to honour Jeanne Alice in his naming of the rose given her status and as being the wife of a French hero.

By all accounts the couple had a glittering social life, even representing their country at Queen Victoria's Diamond Jubilee in London in 1896.

The rose 'Duchesse d'Auerstädt'

Type of rose: Noisette
Introduced: 1888
Breeder: Bernaix, Lyon, France
Parentage: Sport of *Rosa* 'Rêve d'Or'
Other names: *Rosa* 'Mme la Duchesse d'Auerstaedt'

Graham Stuart Thomas, the "gentleman" of old roses, states that this is a valuable variety. It is a little-known sport of 'Rêve d'Or', itself a wonderful golden rambler. The flowers are fully double, with an interesting and intense colour of buff, apricot and gold. The buds are tight and comparatively small when compared with the size of the blooms, with deeper hues. The blooms are striking, with their subtle colour and conformation, quartered and full. They are intensely fragrant, with that delicious scent reminiscent of tea.

Like most Noisettes, this rose is vigorous, with foliage that is large and a soft, dull green. She is relatively thornless, her flowering stems are long, and her new growth a delicious purple, which sets off her blooms.

Although the respected plant reference "Botanica" states she is spring-flowering with some autumn re-bloom, here in our garden in New Zealand, given fair weather, she is a mass of buds tinged with greenish lemon even in high summer. She dislikes the wet, and her buds will ball and fail to open in rainy conditions.

Alexandre Bernaix (1831–1905), her breeder, began his career in Villeurbanne-Lyon in 1869 and eventually his nursery became the largest in Lyon – then the biggest rose-growing area in France. He bred his roses, some forty or so, between 1886 and 1897; all are fine plants. His best-known variety is the delicious and flamboyant climbing Tea rose 'Souvenir de Mme Léonie Viennot'.

Zoé, Comtesse du Cayla

1785–1852

From an early age Zoé Victoire Talon, who would become the Comtesse du Cayla, was caught up in the background treachery and secret politics of the French Revolution, and she was to become a lifelong royalist. Her mother, Jeanne-Agnès-Gabrielle, Comtesse de Pestre, came from a respected legal family, while her father, Antoine Omer Talon, was magistrate and advocate to King Louis XVI.

In 1789, when the French Revolution erupted, Talon was lieutenant of the Châtelet in Paris, in charge of its court, police headquarters and prison. In this role he was involved in the notorious trial of the Marquis de Favras. The Marquis was accused of conspiring to take the King and his family out of France, install Louis-Stanislas-Xavier, the Comte de Provence (later Louis XVIII), as regent and re-establish an absolute monarchy. The Marquis de Favras was hanged for treason in February 1790 and the records of the trial disappeared, so it was thought possible that Talon had been influential in concealing the involvement of the King and Comte de Provence.

It was a time of spies and subterfuge, as royalists worked behind the cover of cooperation with the revolution to aid the royal family – but also, often, to line their own pockets. Talon, with his uncle, Maximilien Radix de Sainte-Foix, was part of what became known as the Secret Committee of the Tuileries, a web-like coalition of political and financial interests who carried on a clandestine correspondence with the King.

In 1792, just after Zoé's seventh birthday, her father's secret letters were discovered and a warrant for his arrest was issued. However, Talon evaded capture, fleeing first to London and then to the USA, where he made money from the import–export trade. He later returned to France, but was arrested on the orders of Napoléon Bonaparte.

Zoé's mother went into hiding herself for a time, and Zoé was sent to the school set up by Madame Campan, Marie Antoinette's former lady-in-waiting. Located in St Germain-en-Laye near Paris, the school drew the daughters of the French nobility, but Madame Campan also educated the Bonaparte children, including Hortense de Beauharnais, the daughter of Empress Joséphine. Zoé was brought to the school by the Comte de Scépeaux, who begged that she be taken in. It was recorded that in 1800,

Zoé Talon, Comtesse du Cayla, with her two children, Ugoline and Ugolin, on the terrace of Château Saint-Ouen in 1825 by Baron François Pascal Simon Gérard (1770–1837).

aged fourteen, Zoé went to a masked ball held by Madame Campan, for which she controversially dressed as an old cake seller.

Zoé married Achille de Baschi, Comte du Cayla, in 1802, and they had two children, Ugolin and Ugoline. In her letters, Zoé wrote often of her brother Denys Talon, who became an officer in the army, fighting in the campaigns in Italy, France and Russia, and who chose all her horses for her.

The Comtesse du Cayla became a part of the "club" of French aristo-crats living in the Faubourg Saint Germain, who were close to the royalist cause. The Faubourg was the neighbourhood around the Boulevard Saint Germain, on the Left Bank of the river Seine, where the fashionable nobil-ity had chosen to build their grand mansions. Zoé counted among her friends the influential politician Talleyrand and Viscomte Sosthène de la Rochefoucauld, an *aide de camp* to the future Charles X. But she was also on good terms with members of the Bonaparte household, in particular Hortense de Beauharnais.

In her memoirs, Hortense confided later, after the restoration, that the Comtesse "had always shown me the warmest friendship. And in spite of recent events continued to come and see me and did not hide her joy at the return of the Bourbons. I thought this feeling very natural."

A history of the political salons of the era and Zoé's involvement in them identifies that, in the winter of 1813 to 1814, the future king received Zoé at his court-in-exile, at Hartwell House in Buckinghamshire, England. This was where he lived from 1808 until after the restoration of the French monarchy in April 1814. She had been sent by the nobles of the Faubourg to discuss Louis's return to rule France, and travelled secretly, claiming that she was going to Holland for the sake of her health.

The ambitious, highly political and manipulative Louis, Comte de Provence, was the younger brother of Louis XVI. He took the title of king on the death of his nephew, but did not rule France until after Napoléon's abdication in 1814. His sister, Madame Elisabeth, records: "My brother, the Comte de Provence, is the most enlightened of advisers. His judge-ment on men and things is seldom mistaken, and his vast memory supplies him with an inexhaustible source of interesting anecdotes." She also noted that: "He kept himself out of danger and reserved himself for the future."

In 1817, Zoé's separation from the Comte du Cayla was supported both by her mother-in-law – who had been a lady-in-waiting to the Comtesse de Provence – and by the King: the man who would come to consider her his favourite mistress.

Comtesse Zoé du Cayla was described as seductive, intelligent and rather fierce. When Louis XVIII became more closely acquainted with her after 1817, he was in desperate need of a friend he could trust. She became that friend and was granted the rarest and most enviable honour – a "correspondence". She wrote daily to him, letters that were used by friend and foe as a conduit to Louis. Sosthène de la Rochefoucauld, an ultra-royalist, is thought by some to have deliberately positioned Zoé as mistress to the King, who was more liberal than these right-wing sections of the nobility. Louis's younger brother, the Comte d'Artois and future King Charles X, used her to regain entry into Louis's confidence, and she was seen as influential in securing royal favours.

However, it appears that Zoé was less interested in shaping the course of French politics than in enjoying the good life. What started as a love affair became a genuine friendship. Louis carefully regulated visiting times for mistresses and officials, and every Wednesday from three until six in the afternoon Zoé visited him, with orders from Louis that they were not to be disturbed.

As a charming, amusing, agreeable companion for an ageing invalid, she used her growing influence to secure her position and her wealth against the time when Louis died. He designed and built her a home at Saint-Ouen, demolishing the existing château north of Paris and laying the first stone with her. He planned her parties and showered her with gifts, furniture and money. He gave her a magnificent service of Sèvres porcelain, lavishly gilded and painted with detailed scenes of the new Château de Saint-Ouen and its gardens.

After the death of Louis XVIII in 1824, Zoé became involved in her farm and was successful in her attempts to improve the quality and breeding of French sheep. She remained at the mansion Louis designed for her at Saint-Ouen until she died nearly thirty years later.

The rose 'Comtesse du Cayla'

Type of rose: China
Introduced: 1902
Breeder: Pierre Guillot, Lyon, France
Parentage: Rosa 'Rival de Paestum' x Rosa 'Mme Falcot'

'Comtesse du Cayla' is perhaps the best of a dozen or so China roses introduced to the market in Edwardian times. She is a charming rose with semi-double, nodding flowers of orange and pink with red highlights. The colours vary depending on the weather, but she shows off all her bright finery when the fully open blooms appear to dance on the bush like butterflies. Unusually for a China, this rose is highly scented and repeats well.

She is of discreet height, barely a metre tall, with sparse, dark green foliage that shows itself as dark plum when young. There is a sense of lightness about this rose in the garden, and if a rose could be called witty, then this is the one, with her vibrant flash of quick subtlety as she blooms.

The family nursery of Guillot et Fils, in particular Jean-Baptiste André Guillot, the second rose grower in the family, is credited with breeding the first Hybrid Tea, 'La France', and also discovering the process of budding seedlings of the dog rose Rosa canina as understock, so enabling the commercialisation of roses. Prior to this, the plants were propagated by cuttings, which was costly in terms of the amount of mother wood required. His son, Pierre Guillot (1855–1918), joined his father's business in 1884 and produced forty-one roses.

Marie Louise, Grand Duchess of Parma

1791–1847

The marriage of Marie Louise of Austria to the French Emperor Napoléon I did not begin auspiciously. She was his second wife, the grandniece of the much-maligned Marie Antionette and, when she heard she was being suggested as a match for the newly divorced Napoléon, she begged her father not to allow it.

Baptised Maria Ludovica Leopoldine Franziska Theresa Josepha Lucia, Marie Louise was the daughter of the Holy Roman Emperor Francis II, of the House of Habsburg. The eighteen-year-old regarded with horror the prospect of marrying Napoléon and although she objected at being sacrificed to protect Austrian interests, she complied when she was persuaded that the security of her country depended upon this marriage.

Her acceptance indicated her quiescent and obedient nature: "The will of my father has consistently been mine; my happiness will always be involved in his. It is in these principles that the Emperor Napoléon cannot fail to find a pledge of the sentiments which will actuate my conduct towards my husband; happy if I can contribute to his happiness, and to that of a great nation. I give, with the permission of my father, my consent to my union with the Emperor Napoléon." Eager to secure his prize, Napoléon rode out to claim her before the official ceremony, which was set in the chapel of the Louvre Palace in the spring of 1810. The formalities were then conducted by proxy without the Emperor in attendance.

The young Marie Louise was compared unfavourably with the worldly Joséphine, Napoléon's first wife, and ridiculed by the court and the French people. She was not a beauty, but modest, innocent and unambitious, her personality as yet undeveloped. However, for Napoléon, she provided ascendance to the ranks of the ruling European aristocracy, which he craved. He tolerated her shyness, lack of wit and political insight, and inelegant dress, but he also needed her to produce the heir to the Napoleonic dynasty that Joséphine had been unable to give him.

Despite her initial reluctance, Marie Louise came to adore her husband and their letters portray a mutual love. His feelings for her were expressed rather dramatically when, during her difficult labour with their first and only child in 1811, Napoléon told the doctors that if there was a

Detail from a nineteenth-century portrait of Marie Louise, showing her with her son Napoléon François, the King of Rome, by Baron François Pascal Simon Gérard (1770–1837).

choice between the lives of his wife and his son, then she should be spared. The child, Napoléon François, given the title King of Rome, was delivered safely, and Marie Louise's position by the Emperor's side was secured. He gave her a 275-carat diamond necklace as a token of his love.

Napoléon kept Marie Louise cloistered from any unsupervised contact, especially with men, but after giving him an heir to the French empire, her life became more tolerable. During Napoléon's absences, Marie Louise was regent, even though she was ill-suited to the role, with no knowledge or understanding of the affairs of state. She disliked being removed from the safety of the women's quarters. She easily became a pawn in the ambitions of the power-hungry, who found a way to her through her chief lady-in-waiting, the Duchesse de Montebello. Apart from the Duchesse, her life was dominated by overbearing men: her father, Napoléon, and her consort and second husband, Adam Adalbert, Count von Neipperg.

By 1814, Napoléon's forces had been pushed back into France by the Allies – a coalition of Russia, Austria, Prussia, the UK, Sweden, Spain and several German states. As the Allies approached Paris, Marie Louise fled to Blois in the Loire valley, and was joined by Napoléon's brothers. Although she supported Napoléon throughout his travails, she refused to join him in exile on Elba. She wrote to him there, and in a letter from Aix-en-Savoie on 3 August 1814 declares: "I am pleased with Count [von] Neipperg, whom my father has appointed to attend on me, he talks about you so pleasantly and in a way which goes straight to my heart, for I need to talk about you during this cruel absence. When, I wonder, shall I be able to see you again and embrace you? I long for it so much, and shall only be happy and contented when I can tell you with my own lips that I love you very tenderly."

She never saw Napoléon again and her exile in Parma, arranged by the Allies, also deliberately separated her from her son. The young Napoléon François was kept in Austria with Marie Louise's father; she would visit him once more – as he lay dying from tuberculosis, aged twenty-one.

Four months after Napoléon's death in 1821, Marie Louise married Count von Neipperg, who had escorted her to Austria after the Emperor's abdication. Initially a spy for her father, Francis II, watching and influencing Marie Louise on his behalf, he became the only man she trusted. She had two children, Albertine and William, from her affair with the Count, and a third, Mathilde, after their marriage; the Count died in 1829.

The former Empress of France became a reforming ruler of the Duchy of Parma, the elegant northern Italian city. She died there aged fifty-six.

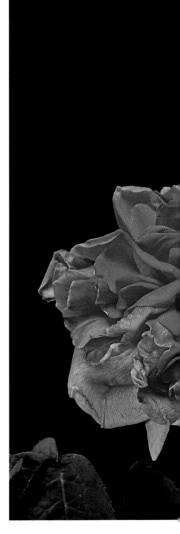

The rose 'Marie Louise'

Type of rose: Damask
Introduced: c.1811
Breeder: Unknown

The ordinary little buds on this rose give no hint of the grandeur that will evolve from them. When open, one succumbs to wonder at the majestic pink, large, double-petalled blooms, overlaid with mauve. The flowers have

a pronounced button eye trying to peep through all the soft glowing petals and are blessed with a delightful sweet perfume. 'Marie Louise' vies for a place, among many contenders, as one of the most sumptuous of flowers.

This tall shrub, almost devoid of thorns, has a good covering of foliage and keeps a special place in our Damask border. The blooms are borne in large clusters on arching canes and, at the height of its flowering season, it becomes

lax, weighed down by their weight. Unlike the Empress, 'Marie Louise' the rose thrives on neglect.

There is some confusion over the genesis of this rose, as there appear to have been three roses bearing the name. Interestingly, it is claimed by some that the true 'Marie Louise' was raised in 1811, the year after the Duchesse's marriage to Napoléon, and was to be found at Malmaison, the home of his first wife Joséphine. The botanical artist

Pierre-Joseph Redouté was commissioned by Joséphine to paint her roses, but the plant in his illustration differs from the rose in our garden, which is the one commonly found in commerce today.

Other rose historians claim it was an existing flower, renamed after Marie Louise, or that the delectable 'Duchesse d'Angoulême' (see pp.94–5) was in fact originally named after Marie Louise. Whatever its true origins, this is a rose not to be missed.

Grace Darling

1815–1842

"Among the dwellers in the silent fields
The natural heart is touched, and public way
And crowded street resound with ballad strains,
Inspired by One whose very name bespeaks
Favour divine, exalting human love;
Whom, since her birth on bleak Northumbria's coast,
Known unto few but prized as far as known,
A single Act endears to high and low ..."

So wrote the celebrated Romantic poet William Wordsworth of Grace Horsley Darling, the daughter of a lighthouse keeper in the Farne Islands, off the wild Northumberland coast of north-east England.

At the age of twenty-two, Grace became a national heroine after she and her father courageously rowed out in ferocious seas to rescue nine survivors stranded on the Big Harcar rocks. She captured the heart of Victorian Britain with her act of bravery and inspired numerous paintings, commemorative plates, biographies, poems and, in 1884, the name of a rose.

The seventh of nine children, Grace lived with her parents William and Thomasin in the Longstone Island lighthouse. She learned to love the sea and its moods, asking endless questions about the coastline and the North Sea's cross-currents, which made shipping so hazardous. In reply to one of her later admirers, she wrote of her life: "I have been brought up on the island, learned to read and write by my parents, and knot, spin and sew; indeed I have no time to spare, but when I have been on the Main I am quite surprised to see people generally after what they call getting their day's work done, they sit down, some play at cards, which I do not understand."

On a stormy night in the autumn of 1838, the steamship *Forfarshire* foundered in heavy seas, leaving nine survivors from its crew and passengers of more than sixty clinging to the rocks. Grace woke early on the morning of

7 September to the sound of roaring wind and spotted the wreck a mile away. It appeared that the lifeboat from Seahouses had not been launched, perhaps because of the rough seas, so she and her father took to the rescue. William needed some persuasion, reportedly uneasy that he had only Grace to help him, but his daughter's insistence prevailed and together they rowed in their flat-bottomed coble to Big Harcar.

William leapt to the rocks, leaving Grace to row furiously against the waves. They saved five souls on their first trip, including a woman who had lost her two children. Three sailors among the survivors helped to row the coble back to Longstone. Grace stayed at the lighthouse, while William and two crewmen rowed back for the remaining four survivors.

News of the rescue spread through the country, becoming more sensational with each telling. The witch-hunt for the ship owners, who were accused of wilfully sailing a disabled vessel, was overshadowed by stories of the heroism of young, pretty Grace. She became a sensation, receiving offers of marriage, requests to paint her portrait, and demands for locks of her hair and pieces of the dress she had been wearing during the rescue.

The nine survivors presented Grace with a lock of hair from each of them in a gold locket. In a letter, Queen Victoria acknowledged her bravery and sent fifty pounds. The Humane Society gave her a gold medal, and a public subscription raised seven hundred pounds for the Darling family. The Duke of Northumberland became her legal protector, setting up a trust for her and advising on "troublesome applications, matrimonial or otherwise". Grace asked for only five pounds every six months.

Grace was uncomfortable with the sudden fame, which threatened to take her away from the life she loved. She rejected many offers of marriage and remained in the Longstone lighthouse. Having developed what was understood to be tuberculosis, she finally left her beloved island, first to stay with friends and then to convalesce with her sister in nearby Bamburgh, where she died in 1842 at the age of twenty-six. Her body was entombed in a mausoleum funded by public subscription, including a donation from Queen Victoria, in the churchyard at Bamburgh. To this day the Royal National Lifeboat Institution names boats in honour of Grace Darling.

FOLLOWING PAGE

A detail from the nineteenth-century painting *Grace Darling Rowing a Coble in Heavy Seas* by Thomas Brooks (1818–1891).

The rose 'Grace Darling'

Type of rose: Hybrid Tea
Introduced: 1884
Breeder: Bennett, England
Parentage: Unknown

*'Grace Darling' is a wonderful, genteel
rose, befitting a Victorian heroine. A
free-flowering variety of low to medium
growth, she expresses herself with her
blooms. At first glance these are a soft
pink, and it is only on closer inspection
that they reveal themselves to be much
more subtle, with tones from deep pink
to cream, fading to almost white. The
flowers are only slightly scented, but
show a quiet refinement rarely seen today
in modern Hybrid Teas.*

*In 1884, 'Grace Darling' captured the
imagination of the Victorians, and the
rose became an instant favourite – one
of the few Hybrid Teas to have endured
over time. She is often described as a
Tea rose, which indicates how close the
relationship between the two families
was in those early years of breeding.*

*Henry Bennett, who introduced this
rose, was a cattle breeder and applied his
knowledge to breeding roses. He advised
growers to use both their brains and their
imagination, then to observe the results
and learn for next time. In 1879, he
amazed the rose world by introducing ten
"Pedigree Hybrids of the Tea rose", a
claim he could prove with records. The
word "pedigree" came straight from the
cattle ring. Hybrid Teas were officially
recognised as a class in 1893, three years
after Bennett's death.*

Anaïs Ségalas

1819–1895

rench poet, dramatist and novelist, committed Catholic and later a supporter of the Second Empire, Anaïs Ségalas was an intellectual and an early feminist who focused on the position of women in nineteenth-century France.

She was born Anaïs Menard, the daughter of Charles Menard from France and Anne Bonne Portier, a creole from Saint-Domingue, on the Caribbean island that is today split between Haiti and the Dominican Republic. When she was only eight, Anaïs surprised her parents with a poem for her father's birthday, revealing her talent. At sixteen, a year after her marriage to Basque lawyer Victor Ségalas, she published her first book of verse, *Les Algériennes*.

Anaïs believed that gifted women had a right to pursue a career of their own, as well as a right to a degree of equality in marriage – and she lived her own life accordingly. Before her marriage, she is said to have made it a condition that she must be allowed to develop her art unhampered by marital conventions.

Her poetic work, published in leading French journals and in her own collections, stressed the contribution of women both socially and domestically. As a fervent Catholic, her poems about women had a serious moral purpose and emphasised the significance of women achieving a better society through sharing love and affection. Her collection *La Femme* (1847) was concerned with how women of different backgrounds could each contribute to society, while the earlier *Les Enfantines* (1844), subtitled "Poems to My Daughter", had a maternal theme. The poem "Bertile" begins with this verse, comparing a new birth to a fresh, new rose:

"See how my house is full of life and gaiety,
And that God also sees it;
The bird of paradise, happiness, comes to swoop down
And sing on my roof.
Yesterday, in my garden, a hatchling flower unfurled
On the freshest rose bush;
Yesterday a beautiful child, another celestial rose,
Was born into my family's heart."

Anaïs Ségalas photographed in the late-nineteenth century by Pierre Petit (1832–1909).

In the mid 1830s she collaborated on *Le Journal des Femmes*, a Christian newspaper that at first called for civil rights and education for women, although those feminist ideals were eventually abandoned and it became a fashion journal.

The February Revolution of 1848, which ended the monarchy of Louis-Philippe and led to the establishment of the Second Republic, would become a turning point in her feminism. At first she attended meetings of the Société de la Voix des Femmes, the political club linked to the feminist daily newspaper founded by Eugénie Niboyet, and offered her work *La Femme* to Niboyet's library of feminist literature. She was also involved in the similarly short-lived Société d'Education Mutuelle des Femmes, which aimed to organise centres of education and co-operative employment for women.

Anaïs had begun to write critical reviews as well for the republican newspaper *Le Corsaire*. She was happy to use her skills supporting the revolution – as long as it promoted harmony among classes, and defence of order, property and religion. Her devout Catholic views distanced her from the more socialist and democratic feminists of the time, especially when they called for civic and political equity and the restoration of divorce. Anaïs kept to the idea that men and women had "separate spheres" – the public and the private – and favoured only a limited broadening of women's rights.

This kind of tension undermined the early and brief feminist movement in France. In the later months of 1848, amid growing disharmony, Anaïs withdrew from feminist circles.

Later, she fully supported the Second Empire, with its call for political and social order and its claim to defend the rights of the Catholic Church. In recognition of this support, she received one of only a handful of complimentary copies of Napoléon III's *Vie de César*.

She retired to her Paris home on the Boulevard des Capucins, where she held a small literary salon. Anaïs continued with her poetry and literary pursuits long after the spark of 1848 French feminism had died. She is buried in the famed Père Lachaise cemetery in Paris, next to her husband and in the company of many other literary figures of her age.

The rose 'Anaïs Ségalas'

Type of rose: Gallica
Introduced: 1837
Breeder: Vibert, Angers, France
Parentage: Unknown

'Anaïs Ségalas' is one of the most prolific of "found" roses in old cemeteries in New Zealand. She has survived a hundred years of neglect, yet still blooms in abundance. She weaves her subtle enchantment throughout our garden and her survival is linked to her enduring health and her ability to sucker freely.

She produces soft purple blooms with slight streaks. Fading to a grey lilac, they are pleasing in their understatedness. Her charm is enhanced by a central green eye that gains prominence as the blooms fade. The beautifully formed flowers, with a strong, heady fragrance, are borne in clusters on a vigorous, dense shrub. The reddish prickles on the canes are a lovely combination with her attractive olive-green leaves. This rose heralds spring in our garden, making it doubly cherished.

There has been some debate about whether this delectable rose is a Gallica or a Centifolia. French Gallica expert François Joyaux places her firmly in the Gallica camp, as does the English authority, Graham Stuart Thomas.

Jean-Pierre Vibert, the breeder, told his grandson shortly: "I love only Napoléon and roses and after all the evils from which I have suffered there remain to me only two objects of profound hatred, the English, who overthrew my idol, and the white worms that destroyed my roses." A prolific and well-respected French breeder, Vibert carried out the first crossings of Gallica roses with the repeat-flowering Chinas, paving the way for a new generation of repeat-flowering roses.

I have wondered why a breeder who loved Napoléon I would acknowledge a woman who supported Napoléon III, whom Bonaparte fans call "Napoléon le Petit". He chose a tough, endearing rose to remember a tough, endearing woman.

Queen Victoria

1819–1901

Alexandrina Victoria was the only child of Edward, Duke of Kent, the fourth son of King George III, and Princess Mary Louise Victoria of Saxe-Coburg-Saalfeld. She was fifth in line to the British throne following her father and his three older brothers. Her grandfather and her father both died in 1820. George IV died in 1830 and as there were no surviving children from her uncles she became heir presumptive on the death of her last uncle William IV, who succeeded George IV. He died in 1837 and therefore a month after her eighteenth birthday, Victoria became the monarch of the UK and Ireland (and in 1876 would add Empress of India).

Woken early in the morning, Victoria received the news that she was now Queen dressed in her night attire. She wrote in her journal: "Since it has pleased Providence to place me in this station, I shall do my utmost to fulfil my duty to my country; I am very young, and perhaps in many, though not all things, inexperienced, but I am sure, that very few have more good will and more desire to do what is fit and right than I have."

The new Queen had led a sheltered and somewhat stifled life under the care of her German-born mother in apartments at Kensington Palace in London. But she emerged from near obscurity as a stark contrast to her uncles: she was a young innocent, viewed romantically by her subjects.

She acted quickly to remove herself from her mother's influence and that of Sir John Conroy, who had tried to gain regency until Victoria was twenty-one. She took firm control with the help of her first prime minister, Lord Melbourne, with whom she had a long and supportive relationship. As the longest-serving of all British monarchs, Victoria encountered ten different prime ministers during her reign, some coming to office more than once.

Victoria married her cousin, Prince Albert of Saxe-Coburg-Gotha, in 1840, though she was initially reluctant to relinquish her independence and unwilling to take on the yoke of a married woman. She was susceptible to male beauty, and cousin Albert was "extremely handsome; his hair is about the same colour as mine; his eyes are large and blue, and he has a beautiful nose and a very sweet mouth with fine teeth; but the charm of his countenance is his expression, which is most delightful; *c'est à la fois* full of goodness and sweetness, and very clever and intelligent".

Queen Victoria, aged only nineteen, shortly after she acceded to the throne, from a portrait by Thomas Sully (1783–1872).

It appears that she fell in love with Albert from their first meeting, and continued to adore him, relying on him throughout their marriage. Albert said of his wife: "Victoria is said to be incredibly stubborn, and her extreme obstinacy to be constantly at war with her good nature." He never failed her, coping with her reputedly terrible temper and mood swings. They were a devoted couple and she a loving wife and mother to their nine children. Serene and radiant in her happiness, she was also formidable, stoical, calm and determined. She could be fiercely furious at anything that displeased her.

Although Albert suffered indifferent health, with bouts of depression and fatigue, he became immersed in matters of state and influenced her reign greatly. He lent his support to reforming causes, including welfare, university education and the ending of slavery, and ensured the success of the Great Exhibition of industry and culture in 1851. Albert died in 1861, aged forty-two, leaving Victoria a widow at the same age. The diagnosis at the time was typhoid fever, but modern assessments suggest he may have been suffering with a chronic disease, perhaps even cancer. A veil of grief descended over Victoria for the rest of her life.

She had been so guided by the Prince Consort that, after his death, she said: "I am anxious to repeat one thing, and that one is my firm resolve, my irrevocable decision, viz. that his wishes – his plans – about everything, his views about everything, are to be my law! And no human power will make me swerve from what he decided and wished."

She was miserable while doing her government duties and remained secluded from London at Windsor Castle and the two homes she and Albert had made together, at Osbourne House on the Isle of Wight and Balmoral Castle in Scotland. There was much criticism when she took refuge behind her widowhood and, in her absence, the republican movement, which sought to remove the monarchy, grew stronger. In a letter to her friend, the poet and author Theodore Martin, she wrote: "It is not the Queen's sorrow which keeps her secluded … It is her overwhelming work and her health, which is greatly shaken by her sorrow, and the totally overwhelming amount of work and responsibility …"

In 1871, after the establishment of the Third Republic in France the previous year, British republicanism was at its height. The tenth anniversary of Albert's death was nearing, and Victoria's eldest son Edward, the Prince of Wales, was ill with typhoid fever. She feared he would die, just like his father. But Edward recovered, and she and her son embarked on a rejoicing public parade through London in February 1872. This, and an incident two days later, when a young man brandished an unloaded pistol at her carriage, helped to revive positive public feeling for the Queen.

Victoria died at the age of eighty-one, gently failing of old age, with her family around her. Her reign had spanned momentous, terrible and contentious events, from the Great Famine following the potato blight in Ireland in 1845 and the European revolutions of 1848, to the establishment of British colonial rule in India in 1858, the publication of Charles Darwin's *On the Origin of Species* in 1859, the Anglo-Zulu War in 1879 and the coming of the railway age.

She was buried next to her beloved Albert, in the Frogmore Mausoleum in the grounds of Windsor Great Park where, as a widow, she had spent so much time seeking solace and strength.

A detail from a painting by Sir Edwin Landseer (1802–73), entitled *Windsor Castle in modern time*; Queen Victoria, Prince Albert and Victoria, Princess Royal (1840–43).

The rose 'Reine Victoria'

Type of rose: Bourbon
Introduced: 1872
Breeder: Schwartz/Labruyère, Lyon France
Other names: *Rosa* 'La Reine Victoria'

'Reine Victoria' has an elegant charm completely at odds with her namesake. Her blooms are borne well aloft, fully globular and fragrant, with fragile petals reminiscent of thin shells. The flowers have a delicate and silky texture; a rich, silvery, rose pink, they are paler within and at the base.

This is a delightful rose, growing to a slender two metres in height. She has long canes, suitable for weaving through a trellis or obelisk, with soft, matte green leaves. She flowers profusely in the spring and the blooms are then spasmodic in the autumn. Like Queen Victoria, she likes the best conditions; she may be difficult in anything but the richest soils.

Graham Stuart Thomas, in his book "The Old Shrub Rose", says of 'Reine Victoria' and her lighter-coloured sport, 'Mme Pierre Oger', that "I know of no other roses with more delicate charm. They are unique period pieces."

'Reine Victoria' is attributed to two growers in late-nineteenth-century Lyon, and sometimes to both. Joseph Schwartz (1841–1885) took over the business of Jean-Baptiste Guillot (1803–1882), known as Guillot Père, after Guillot's son, also called Jean-Baptiste, left to set up his own nursery. Schwartz produced his roses between 1871 and 1885, after which the business was continued first by his wife, and then by their son. Eugène Labruyère's roses were introduced from 1872 to 1874, and his widow released a rose named after her husband in around 1885.

Julie, Baroness Rothschild

1830–1907

Caroline Julie von Rothschild was born in Frankfurt, the daughter of Anselm and Charlotte Rothschild. She was considered by her family to be good-natured and kind, not conventionally pretty, but she had great style and good artistic taste.

Julie, as she was known, and her seven siblings enjoyed the company of writers, artists and composers who were regularly invited to their family home in Vienna. Brought up in a cultural environment with many soirées, dinners and parties, they were a talented bunch of children and many of them went on to excel in their chosen fields. Julie and her younger sister, Sara, charmed visitors with their graceful and beautiful figures and distinguished appearances. They also courted controversy in their enjoyment of smoking cigars, a daring thing for young women to do in the mid 1800s.

The Rothschild family was of German-Jewish origins and, from the late eighteenth century, built up a network of banks and finance houses across Europe. Julie was the great-granddaughter of Mayer Amschel Rothschild, founder of the dynasty. Mayer's sons moved throughout Europe, each setting up a banking business, linked through their family partnership. Julie, of the Austrian house, was engaged to her cousin Adolphe, from the Naples branch; they married in 1850. Adolphe much admired Julie's ability in collecting French *objets d'art*.

He was the Rothschild banker in Naples, not much interested in the tedium of banking or business, and took the opportunity to leave the city after Francis II, King of Sicily and Naples, was forced into exile. Francis's kingdom had stretched across the southern half of Italy, but in 1860 the Italian nationalist and commander Giuseppe Garibaldi led a revolt against him during the Risorgimento, or unification of Italy.

Adolphe and Julie settled in Switzerland, living in the magnificent home they had built on the banks of Lake Geneva. Château de Rothschild, Prégny, was designed in the style of Louis XVI and housed their artefact collections. It may also have had a studio for Julie, a keen photographer.

Like their cousin Béatrice Ephrussi de Rothschild, who created a botanical garden at her villa at Cap Ferrat on the southern French coast, they also collected animals and plants. A hothouse in the garden was

Caroline Julie Rothschild (known to her family as Julie) in a photograph taken in 1864.

arranged by countries and climates, and became much visited by the rich and famous. It is now part of the Geneva Botanical Gardens.

Empress Elisabeth of Austria was a frequent visitor who dined in high style at the château, where a concealed orchestra played in the background. Her last engagement was there, dining with the Rothschilds the evening before she was assassinated, a mere fifteen hours later, on 10 September 1898. She was stabbed by a young anarchist as she walked along the shores of the lake to board a steamship for Montreux.

In 1868, Julie and Adolphe established another home in the elegant 8th arrondissement of Paris, in a house built for Isaac Péreire, whose banking business was a rival to the Rothschild financiers and whose wife also has a rose named after her.

The Rothschilds left their mark not only in art and gardens but in something much more significant: the eye clinics in Paris and Geneva. Returning home one day in an open railway carriage, Adolphe was struck by a tiny coal particle, which lodged in his eye. In Geneva, he sought relief from a young ophthalmologist, who performed a rapid and painless operation to remove the particle. This event prompted Adolphe to set up the Hospital Opthalmique Adolphe de Rothschild in Geneva.

The clinic offered free treatment for patients regardless of their religion or national background. It opened in 1874 as a private institution for the benefit of the community, with Adolphe paying all costs himself. Its articles stated that "the dignity of all patients be maintained regardless of their position". The clinic was to be devoted to the treatment and wellbeing of its patients rather than to research, and Julie was adamant that "the clinics should not become a branch of the Medical Academy".

The Rothschilds later set up a similar clinic in Paris, but it was Julie who worked to establish it, following the death of her husband in 1900. She tackled the project quickly, with vigour and commitment, during a volatile period of anti-Semitism in France. The clinic was opened in 1905.

Julie died childless two years later, and the bulk of her estate was left to her favourite nephew, Maurice. A libertine and gambler, he was the family's black sheep, and was just twenty-six years old when he inherited the château and its treasures. Julie's brother Albert inherited the hospital, which he signed over to the charitable Fondation Ophthalmologique Adolphe de Rothschild. The hospital now works with the Service Publique Hospitalier. In spite of Julie's misgivings, it began to undertake medical research and was responsible for pioneering laser eye surgery in 1978.

The rose 'Baroness Rothschild'

Type of rose: Hybrid Perpetual
Introduced: 1868
Breeder: Pernet, Lyon, France.
Parentage: Sport of Rosa 'Souvenir de la Reine d'Angleterre'
Other names: Rosa 'Baronne Adolphe de Rothschild'

Now simply known as 'Baroness Rothschild', this rose was originally named 'Baronne Adolphe de Rothschild'. She is one of the most beautiful of the Hybrid Perpetual family, which emerged from a complex breeding programme in the 1830s.

'Baroness Rothschild' has undoubted grace and charm, with large, full, pink flowers, slightly cupped when open. The petals are a soft, clear rose pink with a silken texture. Unlike some in her family, she repeats her flowering well, but has only a faint scent, unkindly described by some as being like that of a cowslip.

The bushes are sturdy and well covered with large, grey-green foliage. Hybrid Perpetuals need some care to keep them clean, but nevertheless have a place in the historical lexicon of rose breeding as a significant movement towards repeat-flowering roses. The family is not completely perpetual-flowering, although it does have some degree of repeat.

Hybrid Perpetuals, with their big, buxom flowers, led the field in exhibition roses throughout the reign of Queen Victoria (see pp.126–131). In general, I am diffident about the merits of this family as garden plants in our spray-free garden, as they are not entirely healthy and lack some subtlety.

Joseph Pernet, the grower, eventually merged his business with fellow breeder Ducher in 1881, producing many fine roses. When he married Ducher's daughter, Pernet blended two of the premier French rose families. The unrivalled Pernet–Ducher empire faded

only following the deaths of their two sons during the First World War.

Our rose, grown and marketed as 'Baroness Rothschild', should not be confused with the one described by Dame Miriam Rothschild in her delightful book "The Rothschild Gardens" (1997). There she talks about Rosa rothschildii (Druce, 1913), discovered by George Claridge Druce at Ashton Wold, home of Charles Rothschild, Miriam's father. Bright pink, it was thought to be a variety of Rosa tormentella and later a variety of Rosa obtusifolia. It has now been decided that this beautiful rose is in fact a hybrid of Rosa canina and Rosa sherardii.

Marie-Henriette, Duchesse de Brabant

1836–1902

"If God hears my prayers, I shall not go on living much longer." This cry from the heart of Duchesse Marie-Henriette, a mere five weeks after her wedding to Leopold, Duc de Brabant, the future King Leopold II of Belgium, gives an indication of her despair at their marriage.

Leopold I, the first king of the new state of Belgium, arranged the union between his eighteen-year-old son and heir and Marie-Henriette Anna, the daughter of Joseph, Habsburg Archduke of Austria. The King had also instigated the planning for the earlier wedding of his niece Victoria, Queen of Great Britain, and Albert of Saxe-Coburg-Gotha – a match that proved to be much happier in its fulfilment than that of his son.

They were married in 1853, a day before Marie-Henriette's seventeenth birthday, but they loathed each other on sight and the marriage was generally a disaster. Nevertheless, they did manage to have four children. Their only son died at the age of nine, and after the birth of their third daughter they lived mostly apart: "The King was furious and refused to have anything to do with his admirable wife," according to their first daughter, Louise.

Initially disliked and criticised by her new family, she was described by Leopold as being "of average height, a little chubby, not too pretty but not ugly either, with a barnyard laugh". After 1865, when Leopold came to the Belgian throne, she soon endeared herself to her people as a stable and prudent queen – "the rose of Brabant". Considered by her subjects as having a serene and "elevated" character, she was an accomplished artist and musician. A fine horsewoman, she sought solace in her horses, which she trained herself, and she escaped the constraints of the palace by riding every day. Her ability with horses led to her friendship with the Minister of War, who would sometimes invite her to lead his practice cavalry charges.

Marie-Henriette's indefatigable benevolence and compassion to those around her was confirmed when she volunteered to escort her mentally ill sister-in-law, Charlotte of Belgium, back to her home country. Charlotte's husband had been executed in Mexico and she was being held by the Austrian Habsburgs in Trieste. Marie-Henriette determinedly manipulated her way through the maze of Austrian political intrigue without becoming discouraged and then devoted much time and energy to caring

A portrait of Marie-Henriette
(1863–5) by Franz Xaver
Winterhalter (1805–1873).

for and supporting Charlotte. When the Queen found Charlotte she wrote: "She looked pathetically pleased to see me, all skin and bone and terrified of everyone and everything."

Leopold scandalised and terrorised both his family and the European community, and brought devastation to the Free State of Congo, which had been set up in effect as his own private fiefdom in 1885. He tormented his wife and children with his affairs and shocked everyone with his notorious behaviour. His reputation for buying the favours of young prostitutes brought misery and disgrace. He was named in an English court as a client who had spent eight hundred pounds a month on procuring girls as young as ten. In the Belgian Congo he ruled brutally for his own financial benefit and largely through mercenary forces. His ruthless regime caused much suffering and the deaths of millions of inhabitants.

Estranged from her husband and unable to see her children, Marie-Henriette died in 1902 at her house in the Belgian town of Spa, where she had retired after separating from him. Leopold's behaviour with his three daughters, whom he rejected, was upsetting and today seems inexplicable: Stéphanie was unable to attend her mother's funeral because her father refused to see her; he confined Louise to a mental asylum, although she was perfectly sane; and the youngest, Clémentine, fell in love with Victor Napoléon but had to wait until her father's death before she was able to marry. Having disinherited his daughters, in his greed he pursued litigation against them to have sole claim to his wife's fortune.

After Marie-Henriette's funeral Leopold continued to behave shamelessly. At the age of sixty-five, he was flagrantly open in his affair with the sixteen-year-old Caroline Lacroix, whom he married on his deathbed some nine years later. Such a besieged woman as Marie-Henriette, Duchesse de Brabant, fully deserves a rose to be named for her. This rose in its beauty defies the descriptions of her life at the hands of her monstrous husband.

The rose 'Duchesse de Brabant'

Type of rose: Tea
Introduced: 1857
Breeder: Bernède, France
Parentage: Unknown
Other names: Rosa 'Comtesse de Labarthe', Rosa 'Comtesse Ouwaroff', Rosa 'Shell'

This is a most wondrous rose. Existing in both bush and climbing form, shapely and free flowering, and with a spreading habit, 'Duchesse de Brabant' bears flowers of a clear pink, that are almost translucent. No other petals have quite the pearl-like sheen of this Duchess. The blooms are shaped like tulips and the foliage is light green and pointed. She has one of the best fragrances of all the Teas, a delicious blend of wild rose and tea.

Fortuitously, we received a climbing 'Duchesse de Brabant' in error one year and were stunned and eventually amazed at the beauty and vigour of this rose. It is "stop in your tracks" breathtaking and climbs up and over an arbour, where the blooms can display themselves freely. I am ever grateful for that mistake!

As with many of the Teas, she needs a warm climate to give her best and she is disease free in our garden. The rose was also called 'Comtesse de Labarthe' and 'Comtesse Ouwaroff', and 'Shell' in Bermuda. Whether the Duchesse de Brabant also had these titles is unclear. This was reputedly the favourite flower of US President Theodore Roosevelt and he usually wore one in his buttonhole.

Gertrude Jekyll
1843–1932

Garden designer Gertrude Jekyll was at heart and in her temperament an artist. She is best remembered for the design of her herbaceous borders, which she elevated to become the expression of the quintessential English garden. In her definitive book, *Colour in the Flower Garden* she wrote: "I am strongly of the opinion that a quantity of plants, however good the plants may be in themselves and however ample their number, does not make a garden; it only makes a collection."

She drew heavily on the links between painting and gardening. For her, garden design was creating pictures with flowers. Sensitive to colour, texture and form, her ability to visualise her canvas in three dimensions, not with paints but with plants, indicates how great an artist she was.

Gertrude was born in London, her father was a former captain of the Grenadier Guards and her mother a musician well enough regarded to have studied with Mendelssohn. When Gertrude was a child, the family moved to Bramley in rural Surrey and she grew up single minded, determined and highly artistic. She broke with the usual conventions of middle-class England by enrolling herself at the South Kensington School of Art, one of only a handful of women to do so. Here her ability as an artist was nurtured. Not content with just painting, she developed an interest in woodcarving, silverwork, furnishings and embroidery.

During her studies, she met and was influenced by William Morris, the central figure of the Arts and Crafts Movement. She admired the Pre-Raphaelite painters and later acquired a painting by Dante Gabriel Rossetti. She also adhered to the writing and thinking of the art critic John Ruskin.

Graham Stuart Thomas recounts a meeting with her in her garden: "Pick a piece of anything you would like to talk about and come back and have some tea with me," she told him. Not only was she witty, intelligent and generous, she was also well travelled, visiting Europe, the Middle East and North Africa, and became a gifted plantswoman, as well as a practical gardener. In the 1870s she began to exhibit her artwork, but she suffered from progressive short-sightedness and, as her sight deteriorated, had to lay aside her ambitions in art and embroidery. Undaunted, she took to expressing her art through gardening.

Gertrude Jekyll painted in 1920 by Sir William Newzam Prior Nicholson (1872–1949).

When Gertrude's father died in 1876, the family moved to Munstead in Surrey. Her mother had a house built for them on the heath and Gertrude designed the garden. Soon, she was sought out by horticultural experts and spent forty years in garden design. She became associated with influential artists and thinkers, and wrote prolifically, teaching her readers rather than humouring them, with a lyrical and unselfconscious style.

In 1927 she wrote: "If the ways of gardening that seem to me the most worthy, and that I have tried to give some idea of in my books are found to be of use to others, it is because I have never written a line that was not accounted for by actual hard work and experience … My interest in and devotion to the fine arts has always been one of my keenest joys, and with a love of nature, with all its beauties and wonder."

Gertrude Jekyll was responsible for the modern "mixed border", where roses grow freely with other plants, rather than on their own in formal rose beds with bare stems exposed to the world. She was a gardener of absolute conviction, planting in bold drifts, and earned an international reputation with her botanical knowledge and instincts for colour, light and shade.

She used her own garden at Munstead Wood as her laboratory. In 1889, she met the twenty-year-old architect Edwin Lutyens, and seven years later he designed a house for her, over the road from her mother's. It was the beginning of a partnership that endured in the many great English gardens Gertrude and Edwin created together, such as Hestercombe in Somerset and Castle Drogo in Devon.

Gertrude won the Victorian Medal of Honour and the Veitchian Gold Medal from the Royal Horticultural Society, as well as the White Gold Medal from Massachusetts Horticultural Society. She was also a photographer, an art she took seriously, and developed her own photographs. It was when she first used colour in her photographs that her skill as a gardener became apparent to all.

In her introduction to the chapter "Some Garden Pictures" in *Colour in the Flower Garden*, she expressed her philosophy beautifully: "When the eye is trained to perceive pictorial effect, it is frequently struck by something – some combination of grouping, light and colour – that is seen to have that complete aspect of unity and beauty that to the artist's eye forms a picture. Such are the impressions that the artist-gardener endeavours to produce in every portion of the garden." She has had a lasting influence on gardening styles far beyond England and her influence has been in the design of more than three hundred and fifty gardens.

The rose 'Gertrude Jekyll'

Type of rose: English Rose
Introduced: 1987
Breeder: Austin, Albrighton, England
Parentage: *Rosa* 'Wife of Bath' x *Rosa* 'Comte de Chambord'

This masterpiece of the English Rose family is a great memorial to a great English gardener. She grows tall and slender, into a shrub or small climber. Unlike the reclusive Gertrude, she has flamboyant blooms of a dramatic deep pink – a colour probably never used by Gertrude in her herbaceous borders. She has perfect little buds that open to a fully double rosette that holds its form even in the rain. David Austin says of her: "The buds develop, almost surprisingly, into substantial well-filled rosettes with petals spiralling from the centre, often with the most perfect precision."

Her foliage is grey-green, large and plentiful, with elegant, pointed leaflets. She is described as healthy and a little ungainly. But her most stunning aspect is her fragrance, described as that of the true Damask. 'Gertrude Jekyll' was chosen to produce the first rose perfume in Britain in more than two-hundred-and-fifty years. Plant her in threes where she can stun your eye with her exuberance and beauty. Share a glass of wine with her in the evening and enjoy her fragrance.

David Austin was born on the same farm in Shropshire in central England that now houses the rose business carrying his name. At first he was a farmer, becoming a nurseryman in the 1960s. He attempted in his breeding programme to produce plants with the form and fragrance of old roses, but that had modern characteristics such as repeat flowering and a broader range of colours. 'Gertrude Jekyll' is one of his successes.

Lady Alice Hillingdon

1857–1940

The imposing Lady Alice Marian Harbord-Hamond was the second daughter of the 5th Lord Suffield and grew up in a home surrounded by royalty. Her father was lord-in-waiting to Queen Victoria, and Lord of the Bedchamber to Victoria's son the Prince of Wales, who would later become King Edward VII.

At the age of twenty-eight, Alice married Charles William Mills, the 2nd Baron Hillingdon. Her husband was a banker. From 1885 to 1892, he was also the Member of Parliament for Sevenoaks, in Kent, and he was a Commissioner of Lieutenancy for London. They had three sons: one died as a baby and one perished in action in 1915 during the First World War, leaving the youngest, Arthur Robert Mills, to inherit the title.

This woman with the elegant name and even more elegant rose is recorded in *A Woman's Place: Quotations About Women* by Anne Stibbs as having said: "I am happy now that Charles calls on my bedchamber less frequently than of old. As it is, I now endure but two calls a week and when I hear his steps outside my door I lie down on my bed, close my eyes, open my legs, and think of England." The rose was thereafter described by whimsical nurserymen with a sense of humour as being "good in a bed but better against a wall".

The couple had two country seats: Overstrand Hall, in the village of Overstrand on the Norfolk coast, and the Georgian manor of Wildernesse at Seal in Kent. Charles bought Wildernesse in 1884, enlarging the building and making alterations – adding a gasworks, a laundry and an orphanage. It is now the headquarters of the Royal London Society for the Blind and known as Dorton House.

Overstrand was described as the "village of millionaires" after a newspaper article celebrating its ambience brought the rich and famous there to build their grand country houses. Seven millionaires lived in this small village before the First World War. The estate of Overstrand Hall had been in the Hillingdon family, and was given to Alice and Charles as a wedding present. Lord and Lady Hillingdon had a new manor designed by the architect Sir Edwin Lutyens in the last years of the nineteenth century. With its complex courtyards, Jacobean influences, timbers and flint facings,

Lady Alice Hillingdon, photographed for the Bassano Studio in London in 1921.

Overstrand Hall was described by the architectural historian Nikolaus Pevsner as one of Lutyens' most remarkable buildings. On another property in Overstrand, The Pleasaunce, Lutyens collaborated with the garden designer Gertrude Jekyll.

Alice and Charles also had a property closer to London, in the town of Uxbridge to the north-west of the city. The stately mansion of Hillingdon Court was built by Charles's father, and Lord and Lady Hillingdon became popular figures in the area. They funded a cottage hospital for the local community, while the letters held in The Women's Library at London Metropolitan University record that, in 1909, the Uxbridge Women's Suffrage Society approached Alice to be their president. During the First World War, Lady Hillingdon allowed Overstrand Hall to be used as a hospital for officers, with her sister Bridget as the hospital commandant.

The rose 'Lady Hillingdon'

Type of rose: Tea
Introduced: 1910
Breeders: Lowe and Shawyer, Uxbridge, England
Parentage: *Rosa* 'Papa Gontier' x *Rosa* 'Mme Hoste'

This is an unusual and outstanding rose. Unusual in that her stems and foliage are bronze red when first emerging, and her blooms a soft, subtle apricot. Outstanding because she just oozes charm and class. The fragrance is intriguing, being described by some as freshly opened tea with a hint of apricots. Some people favour it and others are dismissive of its subtle charms.

Her habit is typically Tea, with long, pointed buds, a fragile neck and nodding head. She is certainly refined, and I wonder whether Lady Hillingdon herself was a redhead: her image in the National Portrait Gallery in London is a black-and-white photograph, so gives no clue other than to confirm that her hair was not dark. Her rose blooms continuously and it received a gold medal on its debut in 1910 from the National Rose Society.

The family of Tea roses has an ethereal charm that is missing from the modern descendants. The growth habit is shapely, bushy and luxurious. Her bearing is graceful and she clothes herself in soft, pointed foliage. She grows as a shrub, or as a climber with blooms on stouter necks, which don't hang as gracefully or as shyly as those of the bush variety.

In the early twentieth century, Uxbridge growers Joseph Lowe and George Shawyer operated what is thought to have been the largest cut-flower nursery in Britain at the time, specialising in chrysanthemums for the London flower market. They bred six roses between 1903 and 1913, and 'Lady Hillingdon' was their third release. They named all their roses after people, including Rosa 'Mrs George Shawyer' and Rosa 'Joseph Lowe'.

Ellen Willmott

1858–1934

Ellen Willmott was far more than passionate about gardening. Her obsession was such that she would eventually lose her fortune in the pursuit of it. The clever, headstrong daughter of a wealthy London solicitor was a contemporary of the legendary gardener Gertrude Jekyll. They had a deep respect for each other's abilities in an environment dominated by men, and were the only women awarded the new Victoria Medal of Honour by the Royal Horticultural Society, in 1897.

Born in Heston, in Middlesex, at seventeen Ellen moved to the country estate of Warley Place in Essex. She was able, as a young woman of means, to indulge herself in her favourite pursuits of music (she sang and played several musical instruments) and gardening. Ellen also spoke four languages. She, her younger sister Rose and her mother designed and planted a formal garden until, in 1882, she set forth on her own first gardening adventure, a rock-strewn ravine where she could plant alpines.

As she was single and independently wealthy, with money inherited from her godmother, the Countess Helen Tasker, Ellen was able to indulge her obsession unhindered. In 1888, she further inherited one hundred and forty thousand pounds. She became a hands-on gardener, supported by a fleet of helpers; at one point, she employed some one hundred uniformed gardeners, who provided the workforce for the grounds of her properties.

Ellen was said to be a tyrant – a woman who was imperious and autocratic, who would not tolerate a single weed. She could be wildly extravagant or very mean and was often impossible to deal with. Reputedly she was not terribly likeable and had to strive aggressively for recognition in social and horticultural circles.

She was feckless with her money, giving generous support to plant explorers and throwing her fortune into properties and their gardens in France and Italy. First the Château de Tresserves near Aix-le-Bains in the foothills of the French Alps, which she bought in 1889 after her family's "grand tour" of Europe to celebrate her thirtieth birthday, then Villa Boccanegra, on the Mediterranean coast near Ventimiglia in Liguria, Italy. Her grandiose dreams eventually bankrupted her, but, nonetheless, she had a profound impact on the evolution of gardening.

A twentieth-century portrait of Ellen Willmott by artist Rosa Mantovani.

Ellen funded an expedition to Central Asia and two newly discovered irises were named in her honour, *Iris willmottiana* and *Iris warleyensis*. A peony in her garden, previously not scientifically recorded, was called *Paeonia willmottiae*. In 1894, Ellen joined the Royal Horticultural Society and worked her way into the male-dominated Narcissi Committee, winning gold medals for her daffodils – drifts of narcissi clothed Warley in the spring, and she named her hybrids after her favourite people. She was one of the first women to be elected a fellow of the prestigious Linnean Society, dedicated to the cultivation of the science of natural history.

In spite of her reputation for never sharing plants, Ellen distributed seeds from her garden at Warley each year and her list stood at more than six hundred varieties. She is reputed to have carried seeds of the silver sea holly *Eryngium giganteum* in her pocket and, in the dead of night, to have scattered them in people's gardens. This spiky plant, much like her nature, is now commonly known as "Miss Willmott's Ghost". In her obituary, Sir William Thistleton-Dyer, director of the Royal Botanic Gardens at Kew, wrote: "As gardeners go, she was not considered generous, and one looked carefully at gift plants for fear they might be fearful spreaders."

She was an outstanding plantswoman of her time, a great rosarian and author. Her book *The Genus Rosa*, although a failure when it was first published in 1914, was reprinted under the guidance of the rosarian Graham Stuart Thomas, who did much to restore her reputation. He comments that the book "shows a very real awakening of a great gardener to the manifold beauties of the rose, and a landmark in horticulture history". Many of the original paintings commissioned from Alfred Parsons have been beautifully reproduced in the later edition. Seven roses have been named after her, in addition to the irises, lilies, crocus, primula, lilac and the peony.

Ellen had borrowed money against the success of *The Genus Rosa*, but when that failed to materialise and her French château burned down, requiring expensive restoration, she found herself struggling for funds. Gradually, she began to sell her family heirlooms and properties, and dismiss her gardening staff. During the First World War, her home at Warley was used by the army, wrecking much of the planting.

In her later years, she became fearful and suspicious, and booby-trapped her flowers lest anyone steal them. Warley Place was put up for auction, and her fabled garden vanished through neglect. She died alone with no money, no gardeners or family, sad and bitter but with a legacy of plant varieties and the enduring respect of many horticulturalists.

The rose 'Ellen Willmott'

Type of rose: Hybrid Tea
Introduced: 1936
Breeder: Archer, Kent, England
Parentage: *Rosa* 'Dainty Bess' x
Rosa 'Lady Hillingdon'

Of the seven roses named after Ellen Willmott, our focus is the exquisitely delicate and ethereal Hybrid Tea released two years after her death, the rose with which she is most associated. One other, Rosa willmottiae, was grown from a seed collected in China by Ernest Henry Wilson (see pp.157–8), who was funded by Ellen Willmott. It is recorded as still being available, although not widely grown.

William Archer, though not well known, produced some excellent single roses in the 1930s. The delectable 'Ellen Willmott' is one of his best. He chose a rose that is entirely the opposite of her brusque, imperious manner, perhaps to spite her rather fearsome reputation. It has charming single flowers with pronounced gold and claret stamens centred in a delicate, pale, almost translucent creamy pink. Her petals are

frilled, and the sturdy bush has healthy dark green leathery foliage, with the new leaves being tinged purple. There is nothing sweeter, more beautiful or more gentle than a bloom of 'Ellen Willmott'.

Her seed parent Rosa 'Dainty Bess' is almost identical to her, except for the colour, a soft rose pink. There is nothing in 'Ellen Willmott' to remind us of the apricot Rosa 'Lady Hillingdon' (see pp.146–7), her pollen parent.

Edith Cavell

1865–1915

Born at Swardeston in Norfolk, Edith Cavell was an English nurse and the daughter of a clergyman; she became one of the most enduring heroines of the First World War.

She first worked as a governess, taking a place with a family in Brussels for several years from 1890. Returning home to care for her father during a brief illness, she decided to train as a nurse at the London Hospital. She spent her early career working with typhoid victims in Kent and nursing the poor in Manchester before moving back to Brussels. There, in 1907, when Edith was in her forties, she became the first Head of Nursing at the newly established nursing faculty of the Berkendael Medical Institute. She set up a programme to educate Belgian nurses, until her work radically changed with the declaration of war in 1914.

Edith was at home in England, visiting her newly widowed mother, when the news was announced, on 4 August, that Britain was at war with Germany, following Germany's failure to guarantee that it would respect the neutrality of Belgium. She returned immediately to Brussels, saying to her mother: "I am needed more than ever." She never returned to England.

After the German invasion of Belgium, Edith's nursing school became the Red Cross Hospital, at the disposal of the invading army. Although she was offered the opportunity to return home, she elected to remain with her nurses. She honoured her principles by insisting that all soldiers, no matter what nationality, were treated and nursed with equal attention.

Edith's humanitarian work took a different turn when she started using the hospital as an "underground stop" for British, French and Belgian soldiers escaping from the German army. Edith is credited with helping more than two hundred Allied soldiers escape through neutral Holland. During this period in 1915, Edith said to one of her nursing sisters, a fellow conspirator: "We are bound to get caught one of these days. There are too many people in the organisation and the Germans know that many men are crossing the border." But even that fear did not stop her working with the Resistance.

The Germans were indeed aware of the escapes, and raided the home of Philippe Baucq, a member of the group arranging them. There they found

Edith Cavell poses with a child at Shoreditch Infirmary in 1903.

letters that he had failed to destroy and that incriminated Edith by the mention of her name. The Germans searched the institute but found nothing of substance as Edith had sewn her diary into a cushion, and had burned other papers. The only real evidence they discovered was a tattered postcard from a British soldier, thanking her for helping him reach home.

Edith Cavell was arrested in early August 1915 and was held in a cell for ten weeks. While imprisoned, she admitted to her part in arranging the rescues – possibly because she thought everyone else had already confessed. In October, she stood trial with thirty-four others and was charged with facilitating the escape of enemy subjects into neutral territory. Although this was a breach of military law, it was not a capital offence. However, the German military court wanted to make an example of her. The prosecutor used Edith's confession that she had provided funds and guides to enable soldiers to escape, return to their countries and fight again to argue that she had assisted the enemy. Under military law, she should face the death penalty. Edith was found guilty but the sentence was not passed immediately. Several days later she heard that she had been sentenced to death, along with four others, including Philippe Baucq.

Reverend Gahan, the British chaplain in Brussels, went to visit her shortly afterwards. His visit was documented by the US Ambassador to Belgium at the time: "When Mr Gahan arrived at the prison that night Miss Cavell was lying on the narrow cot in her cell; she arose, drew on a dressing gown, folded it about her thin form, and received him calmly. She had never expected such an end to the trial, but she was brave and was not afraid to die. The judgement had been read to her that afternoon, there in her cell. She had written letters to her mother in England and to certain of her friends, and entrusted them to the German authorities."

Despite last-minute diplomatic efforts to save her, Edith faced the firing squad at 2 a.m. on the following morning, 12 October 1915, proudly wearing her nurse's uniform. Gahan recorded her last statement before the execution: "Standing as I do in view of God and Eternity: I realise that patriotism is not enough. I must have no hatred or bitterness towards anyone."

The speed of her execution and the secretive nature of her trial caused uproar in Britain and the rest of free Europe. The actions of the Germans may have been justified under military law, but it was a serious blunder in terms of public opinion. The death of Edith did not act as a deterrent. Allied recruitment doubled and the morale of the British soared in defiance. This heroic nurse became a worldwide martyr and a clarion call to arms.

The rose 'Edith Cavell'

Type of rose: Polyantha
Introduced: 1917
Breeder: de Ruiter, Netherlands
Parentage: Sport of *Rosa* 'Orléans'
Other names: *Rosa* 'Nurse Cavell'

This small rose has rich red to scarlet clusters of flowers. Fat buds open to flat, semi-double blooms, which continue to appear throughout the season. The tough, sturdy bush sports dark green foliage with stems that are slightly lighter in colour. Some people may bemoan the absence of scent, but she is a worthy rose nevertheless.

Polyantha roses were the supreme bedding plants of the early twentieth century. They are healthy little bushes with clusters of small flowers and look stunning in a hedge.

English rosarian Peter Beales saved Rosa 'Edith Cavell' from extinction. He was asked by the clergyman at Swardeston if he could find some specimens for the village to plant in celebration of the seventieth anniversary of Edith's death, in 1985. A desperate last advertisement for the rose resulted in one gnarled fifty-year-old bush from a garden in Brundall, Norfolk, which produced ten new plants – Edith herself had been rescued and restored to health.

Helen Wilson

*c.*1880–1930

Helen "Nellie" Wilson was the wife of the famed plant hunter Ernest Henry Wilson, who earned the name "Chinese" Wilson for his many exploits in China on plant-gathering missions. She became the first wife to accompany a husband on such trips when she and their daughter joined him on an expedition to Japan in 1914.

Born Helen Ganderton, the shy Nellie – sometimes referred to as Ellen – married Ernest in June 1902 in Edgbaston in Warwickshire, on his return from his first trip to China. At this time the major European powers, along with the USA, were attempting to impose their rule on China. The Empress Dowager Cixi gave her support to a secret society that sought to rid the country of foreign influence. It was named the Boxers after their physical rituals. As the Boxer Rebellion occured, Nellie must have waited anxiously for news of her sweetheart ahead of his return for their wedding.

Their marriage was to be characterised by long absences, as Ernest undertook three further trips to China without Nellie. The couple had to forgo a honeymoon as Ernest, under contract to James Veitch, Britain's most noted nurseryman, was off on his second plant-hunting trip. Among his sponsors was the legendary Ellen Willmott, who urged him into repeated expeditions to the Orient despite his wife's reluctance. Uncompromisingly, Willmott wrote: "It was very sad that such a promising man should be hampered by such an ignorant short-sighted wife at such an early stage of his career."

Nellie's and Ernest's daughter, Muriel Primrose, was born in May 1906 and named after one of his plants from China, *Primula wilsonii*, which flowered for the first time in the Royal Botanic Gardens, Kew, on the day of her birth. This may have marked a turning point in the family's domestic arrangements, but Ernest soon returned to China on behalf of the American organisation the Arnold Arboretum, connected to Harvard University.

He returned in 1909, a few days before his daughter's third birthday – he had last seen her when she was just six months old. The family now moved to Boston, as Ernest was offered work at the Arnold Arboretum. He discovered that he was a minor celebrity there; it was the Bostonians who nicknamed him "Chinese" Wilson. Nellie, however, did not settle happily.

Helen Wilson with her husband Henry and daughter Muriel, in Tokyo, 1914.

In 1910 Ernest was reluctantly persuaded to undertake a fourth expedition to China, reaching a compromise with Nellie, who returned to England, staying with Ernest's family in Birmingham. On this trip he broke his leg when boulders crashed across his path, and he named a bamboo after his daughter: *Sinarundinaria murielae* (now called *Fargesia murielae*). In 1911, the whole family returned to Boston.

Nellie's health was frail and she had spent much of her married life at home, waiting. The couple decided that she and Muriel would join Ernest on his next expedition – to Japan, spending a year photographing forests and nurseries, concentrating in particular on Japanese flowering cherries. Nellie, who suffered chronic bronchitis, spent most of her time in hotels or at the embassy. However, Ernest wrote to his mother: "Everything is novel and interesting, especially to Nellie and Muriel, and both are having the time of their lives. Having them with me makes it much pleasanter and infinitely less lonely for me."

They cut short their trip after Japan entered the First World War, arriving in Boston with treasures – more than six hundred photographs and nearly two thousand specimens – that were then unknown to the West, but that are still grown today.

In 1917, Nellie again accompanied her husband on his sixth and final trip to the Far East, during which he collected a number of important azaleas from the Kurume district of Japan, as well as travelling to Manchuria and Taiwan, and deep into Korea. She and Muriel stayed in Tokyo and Seoul, with Ernest returning between his expeditions. In Korea, they came with him on some of his forays to photograph plant specimens.

There are no remaining letters between Nellie and Ernest, and it has been said that Muriel destroyed them following the death of her parents. So what we know of her comes largely from Ernest's correspondence with his family. It seems that in her unassuming way, Nellie was inordinately proud of her husband's achievements. Ernest, in turn, kept Helen in his mind on his expeditions, naming the first Chinese houseboat the *Ellena* after her, and also, of course, the beautiful white rose, *Rosa helenae*.

In October 1930, just three years after Ernest became Keeper of the Arnold Arboretum, he and Nellie were killed when their car skidded on a wet road as they were travelling home after visiting Muriel. At the funeral, their caskets were covered with flowers and sprays of leaves from plants that Ernest had collected: flowering crab apples and tree honeysuckle, blue beauty berry and the famous handkerchief tree, *Davidia involucrata*.

The rose Rosa helenae

Type of rose: Chinese Synstylae or Musk
Introduced: 1907
Introduced by: Rehder and Wilson

The rosarian Peter Beales classifies this as the foundation rose of a family, while Charles Quest-Ritson in "Climbing Roses of the World" describes it as the eastern counterpart of Rosa brunonii (also known as the Himalayan Musk Rose).

Discovered by Ernest Wilson in 1907 and native to central and southwest China, this is a big scrambling rose for hedges and trees, and it is worthy of its popularity.

In his essay on "Wild Roses: Flowers of the Wayside", Ernest Wilson writes: "Of this type of rose (Rosa moschata) there are half a dozen species native of China now in cultivation. The hardiest of all is Rosa helenae named for my wife. This is a strong growing plant that will make arching canes from six to twelve feet long and produces at the end of short shoots large rounded clusters of pure white, delightfully fragrant flowers to be followed by orange-to-red coloured fruits. The flowers, each about one-and-a-half inches in diameter, have conspicuous yellow anthers and are singularly beautiful. This rose grows fairly well in the Arnold Arboretum but does much better on the limestone soil of Rochester, New York, where, in fact, it is not only hardy but flourishes as on its native heath."

What more can one say? I would only add that it produces wonderful small oval red hips in autumn, which themselves are spectacular.

Constance Spry

1886–1960

Constance Spry, immortalised by David Austin's first English rose, was no ordinary flower arranger. She was an artist who revolutionised floristry with spectacular displays, turning it into an art form. She was also a knowledgeable gardener and called on nature for her inspiration.

Surprisingly, her background was not in gardening but in health education. Connie, as she was known, was born in Derby, in the East Midlands of England, the eldest of six children. Her father was a railway worker who, with the help of night classes, eventually became a headmaster; her mother was the daughter of a shopkeeper. The family moved to Ireland, where Connie trained as a health lecturer. Her first job was as an associate lecturer, teaching first aid and health sciences, and she was appointed secretary of the Dublin Red Cross when the First World War began.

After an unhappy marriage of six years, she moved back to England with her young son Anthony, first to Cumbria, then to London, where she became a teacher. In 1921, she became head of the Continuation School in Hackney, set up to enforce the Education Act of 1918, which decreed that boys and girls between the ages of fourteen and eighteen should attend school one day a week.

Connie was a born teacher, with a clear style of instruction, passing on to her pupils practical skills of cookery and dressmaking. But she saw there were other possibilities when she realised how much pleasure the posies she brought into the classroom gave her pupils. She astounded her family in 1928 when she left teaching to start a career as a flower arranger.

By this time she was involved with Henry Ernest Spry, known as Shav. Connie called herself Mrs Spry and it has always been thought that they married in 1926, but a more recent biography, *The Surprising Life of Constance Spry* by Sue Shephard, suggests there was never a legal wedding. The couple moved to the Old Rectory at Abinger in Surrey. Perhaps, finally, she had the opportunity to set free her artistic flair and follow an interest in flowers that she had cultivated since childhood. Friends in the theatre and cinema world commissioned Connie to create displays for them and then encouraged her to set up a shop. Her first premises, called Flower Decoration, were in Belgrave Road, central London.

A portrait of Constance Spry, painted in 1952 by Mollie Forestier-Walker (1912–1990).

M. Forrester-Walker
1952

Connie had strong views on floristry, modelling her arrangements on the natural form of the garden. Although she gained fame through designing floral arrangements for royalty, including for the wedding of the Duke of Windsor to American divorcée Wallis Simpson in 1937, she also showed ordinary women how to beautify their homes with apparently unassuming plants from their gardens and hedgerows. Connie's philosophy was that flowers could enrich everyone's life, and they should not be reserved for the wealthy. She believed that all you needed to create wonderful arrangements from the simplest of flowers was an imagination. Nothing was too lowly for her arrangements and she used berries, vegetable leaves, twigs and ferns. Her overriding principle was: "Let the flowers remind you of how they are when growing." She also advised: "Do not make lovely flowers into statements of geometry."

Connie loved the rose form, especially the old varieties, and collected and planted many old roses in her garden during a period when their appeal was declining as the modern roses took precedence. No slave to fashion, she used old roses whenever she could, as a not-too-subtle way of increasing their popularity.

In 1934, she opened a second London shop in Mayfair, along with the Constance Spry Flower School and, in 1938, a branch in New York. When the Second World War began, she turned her skills to teaching austerity homemaking. Never one idly to rest on her laurels, in 1946 she founded the Domestic Science School at Winkfield Place, Berkshire. She published thirteen books and many articles on flower decoration.

Her fame and skill as a flower arranger saw her in demand for galas, operas and royal weddings. Connie's style had become so established that she was awarded a royal commission to arrange the flowers for the wedding of Princess Elizabeth to Prince Philip in 1947, and in 1953 she designed the flowers for Westminster Abbey, and the route, for Queen Elizabeth II's coronation, for which she was honoured with an OBE. She and Rosemary Hume, her partner at Winkfield Place, also developed the recipe for Coronation Chicken in the Queen's honour, featuring it in their best-selling *Constance Spry Cookery Book*.

Connie died suddenly in 1960, having slipped on the stairs at Winkfield Place, a year after the formation of the National Association of Flower Arrangement Societies. Her legacy is summed up in her view that: "We want to be born again with new eyes so that we may be newly surprised with the beauty of much to which we have grown blind with custom."

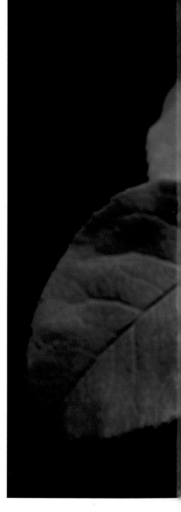

The rose 'Constance Spry'

Type of rose: English Rose
Introduced: 1960
Breeder: Austin, Albrighton, England
Parentage: *Rosa* 'Belle Isis' x
Rosa 'Dainty Maid'

In our garden, this splendid rose grows tall, proud and strong in an ever-increasing mass, greeting visitors with her aloof habit, her blooms nodding above their heads. She astounds with her fragrance, which Graham Stuart Thomas described as being just like

myrrh, after smelling a sample of this prized plant resin. Libby, who worked for us at Trinity Farm, says it is more like disinfected public toilets, but I think that is unkind. 'Constance Spry' has an evocative fragrance of the East, which is rare in roses. This rose was the first in a long line of David Austin roses that carry this unusual perfume.

The blossoms are simply magnificent, in size, shape and colour: a full-blown satiny pink and deeply cupped. They are big, beautiful and generously flowering, with charm, exuberance

and style. I cannot say enough about the generosity of this rose.

The canes are prickly, tall and willowy, swaying gracefully in the spring breeze. The new leaves are a delightful soft pink, darkening with age to deep green. Unlike some of its siblings and descendants, it is remarkably healthy for an Austin rose and adapts well in our spray-free garden. It will climb, arch or sprawl and should never be pruned, but instead allowed to prowl and ramble wherever it wants to go. It has a habit of popping up, unexpectedly, all over the place. A big, bold "lady" of a rose, entirely befitting the big, bold

doyenne of floral architecture, and thankfully entirely lacking in manners.

David Austin bred an entirely new family of roses, which draw their inspiration from the big, full, fragrant old families mingled with the modern remontant, or repeat-flowering, roses. He has produced a hugely diverse family, with varying degrees of success and health. The English Roses have earned a place in history, although not every one will stand the test of time. Of all of them, 'Constance Spry', even though she is once flowering, remains our favourite for her beauty, health, vigour and charm.

Nancy Steen

1898– 1986

As a child, Nancy Steen took her school motto to heart: "*Je sème à tous vents*," it declared: "I sow the seeds of knowledge to the four winds." Today she is remembered in New Zealand as the doyenne of the country's heritage-rose movement, and is recognised the world over as an authority on old roses.

Her parents came to New Zealand in the 1880s, her father from Scottish and her mother from Irish parentage. Originally christened Agnes, after her grandmother, Nancy was described as a diligent and quiet but confident child. Nancy's first job, at an advertising agency in Wellington, gave her creative talents an outlet, but at the age of twenty-eight she trained to become a Karitane nurse, specialising in the care of babies and young children. She married David Steen, a promising accountancy graduate, two years later, and the couple set up home in Auckland. Their daughters, Barbara and Sue, were born in the early 1930s, and Nancy began to discover her interest in gardening, collecting horticultural magazines and catalogues of plants.

While still pursuing her career as a children's nurse, she studied art and developed a special interest in floral drawing. She and David travelled a lot, and Nancy took the opportunity to sketch the flowers and scenery they saw, later creating linocuts from her drawings. One of her proudest artistic achievements was a pictorial alphabet based on New Zealand flora, which was used for teaching. In 1936, Nancy was invited to become a working member of the Auckland Society of Arts, an honour not lightly bestowed. She had a unique combination of talents: a deep botanical knowledge and an artist's eye. Her expertise shone through in the balance she achieved between colour and form.

After the Second World War, during which David was an officer in the Home Service, Nancy and her husband were able to buy a weekend bolt-hole on the fringes of Auckland. Nancy set out with a will to establish her own garden there. Later, she extended her gardening and landscaping skills further, when they built their own home in the city. She designed her garden based on colour themes, and it was here that Nancy's passion for old roses blossomed.

Nancy Steen in her garden with her roses, c.1966.

In her book *The Charm of Old Roses* she writes: "Roses form the background of our garden planning and planting, and, in the main, these old roses are given to us by friends, collected from roadsides and early settlements, or purchased in New Zealand or in England. We are very fortunate in that our present property had most of the essentials we hoped for, sheltered position with a gentle slope to the north, surrounded, but not encroached upon by trees; and a pleasant outlook. The soil was heavy, which was rather astonishing as several hundred yards down the road lies the crater of an extinct volcano."

Old roses have flourished in the temperate New Zealand climate. Not only did the early settlers bring their treasures with them, but records of early nurserymen show that new roses were imported here almost as soon as they were released in Europe. They were planted widely, in hedgerows, cemeteries and old mission houses, and this and their innate toughness have ensured their survival. The treasure trove of heritage roses in New Zealand includes varieties lost elsewhere in the world. As Nancy said: "The more we delve into the history of these fascinating plants, the more our interest in these garden treasures is stimulated."

It was David's love of history that took them driving down the old lanes and byways, recording, gathering and collecting. "Although we have since found many old roses growing semi-wild throughout the country, we shall never forget the excitement of the first discovery," Nancy wrote. She identified that first find as 'Anaïs Ségalas' (see pp.122–5).

Nancy was a total gardener, seeing roses as part of the whole picture. She dug up all her borders every three years to attend to every facet of cultivation – root pruning, shaping and re-nourishment of the soil, the companion plants and the maintenance. She used hops as manure. Her daughter recounts the story of truckloads of warm, beery, fresh hops being delivered to the garden, ensuring that it smelt like a brewery. Nancy and her children would sweep a nearby oak-lined avenue simply to collect the leaves to benefit her compost.

By 1949, she was sought after as a speaker and to write articles for magazines. Requests came in from rose lovers across the world to view her garden. She wrote and designed *The Charm of Old Roses* in 1966, when she was sixty-nine, and we use her book in preference to many newer ones. It was hugely successful, her descriptions of finding roses reading as a fascinating account of a pioneer country. In the introduction she says: "Each year, more and more old roses disappear; so we hope that this record

will serve to remind us of some of the beauties that, of necessity, have had to be swept away – beauties that must have brought a breath of their homeland to lonely pioneers, and particularly to their wives."

She was honoured with life membership of the National Rose Society and, in 1967, recognised by the Dominion Council of the Royal New Zealand Institute of Horticulture as an Associate of Honour. That same year the New Zealand Historic Places Trust asked her to assist with the revised planting of the garden at Kemp House, also known as the Kerikeri Mission House, one of the country's oldest and most historic buildings.

Nancy was a great and consistent supporter of the fledgling Heritage Roses New Zealand organisation, founded in 1980. Apart from her book and her rose, Nancy's other enduring legacy is the Nancy Steen Garden in Auckland, named in honour of her contribution to heritage roses and opened in 1984, two years before she died. Planted by Heritage Roses and the Auckland City Council, it thrives as a fragrant oasis of more than two hundred old-fashioned and species roses.

The rose 'Nancy Steen' ➔

Type of rose: Bush Floribunda
Introduced: 1976
Breeder: Sherwood, Waitara, New Zealand
Parentage: *Rosa* 'Pink Parfait' x (*Rosa* 'Ophelia' x *Rosa* 'Parkdirektor Riggers')

This is a sturdy little rose well suited to the pioneering Nancy Steen. She has fragrant double blooms of a soft blush pink that age to cream. The blooms have a rather informal air about them, sitting in large clusters on a backdrop of dark green foliage. They are produced prolifically throughout the season on a tough, hardy bush.

The rose was bred by George Sherwood, who was at the time president of the New Zealand Rose Breeders' Association and a cattle breeder by profession. Whether it was roses or cows, the formula was the same and "The secret to success is in the breeding," he is claimed to have said. Susan McAffer records in her biography, "The Charm of Nancy Steen", that he wrote to Nancy while she was away on a business trip with David, seeking her permission to name the rose after her. Nancy's daughter responded and gave permission, much to the bemusement of her mother, who worried that she might not like it. When she eventually saw the rose, she was captivated, and was presented with a gold-dipped cluster of the blooms in acknowledgement of her contribution to the growing of old roses, and her diligence and enthusiasm in championing them.

The breeding provides an insight to the strange nature of the hybrid rose. 'Pink Parfait' is a light pink cluster-flowered 'buttonhole' rose, lightly scented. The other parent was a seedling: a cross between the grand old Hybrid Tea 'Ophelia' and a single, five-petalled climber, 'Parkdirektor Riggers'.

The English-bred 'Ophelia' was the prolific ancestor of many great roses. She is a stately marshmallow-pink rose of thirty-five petals, with a fragrance to die for. On the other hand, 'Parkdirektor Riggers' was a red climbing rose from Germany. Its lack of fragrance, and of petals, was offset by an enormously healthy disposition. How, you might ask, could a healthy single red climber wed a deliciously fragrant Hybrid Tea, to produce a seedling that would mate with a buttonhole rose, to produce the delightful 'Nancy Steen'? Such are the ways of hybridisers, who see latent genetic charms and bring them to our gardens.

Ghislaine de Féligonde

1914–1994

There are two versions of the 'Ghislaine de Féligonde' story. The true one was published in the journal of *Roses Anciennes en France*, in an article based on a rare interview with Ghislaine's daughter, and is completely at odds with the legend that has surrounded her for decades.

The legend tells us that this delightful rose was named after a French heroine of the First World War. The story first appears in *The Rose Manual* by Dr J.H. Nicolas of the 1930s, but Jean Turbat, the grandson of breeder Eugène Turbat, retold it many decades later to my husband, Lloyd.

Eugène was one of the trio of famous Orléans nurserymen, along with Barbier and Transon. He was also the president of the French Horticultural Chamber of Commerce and a senator of France. Turbat junior said he had heard the story from his grandfather. It tells of a young officer, the Comte de Féligonde, seriously injured in battle and left in No Man's Land to die, as no one was brave enough to rescue him. His wife, Ghislaine, ventured into the battlefield under the cover of darkness, found him, dragged him to safety and nursed him back to health. She was celebrated as a heroine, thereafter honoured in perpetuity with this beautiful rose.

However, as the real Ghislaine was only two years old when the rose was introduced in 1916, she can hardly be the leading character of this legend. In fact, Ghislaine was the daughter of Comte Charles de Féligonde and Odette de Martel and they dwelt in Paris and Chantemesle, a countryside manor, near Chartres. They often spent holidays at the castle of her maternal uncle Gabriel de St Ferriol, in St Martin d'Uriage, in the alpine south-east of France. He eventually bequeathed this castle to her as his sole heir. The landscape architect Jean-Claude Nicolas Forestier was a friend of the Comte de Féligonde and his wife and also of Eugène Turbat, and it was through Forestier that the rose found its name.

Forestier was an acclaimed designer who went on to create gardens from Spain to Morocco and from New York to Buenos Aires. He was Commissioner of Gardens for the city of Paris and had helped to save the rundown Château de Bagatelle in the Bois de Boulogne, Paris, restoring and remodelling the grounds in the early twentieth century, and adding a

A family photograph of Ghislaine de Féligonde taken in her garden during the 1930s.

rose garden where gravelled walks and trimmed topiary formed the backdrop to more than one thousand five hundred specimens.

Forestier was a rose connoisseur with perfect judgement. In 1907, the rose garden became the venue for the Bagatelle international new rose competition, which has been held there every year since. In 1916, Turbat entered a rose with only a number for identification. It was judged worthy of a Certificate of Merit, but could not receive the award until it had a name. Forestier knew his friends' pretty little daughter and arranged for the rose to be named after her, as its "godmother".

The Comte was indeed severely wounded in battle, but neither his infant daughter nor his wife went to rescue him. Interestingly, many myths and rumours of rescuers and protectors surround the battles of the First World War. Soldiers recorded visions of "angels" who inspired and helped them but, in at least one instance, the source of the rumours could be traced back to a fictional short story – a phenomenon that the literary historian Paul Fussell discusses in his book *The Great War and Modern Memory*. At the Battle of the Somme, with its huge death toll, individuals spoke of Christ-like white helpers or comrades, and it was widely believed among the troops that a band of deserters from both sides had escaped the futility of war by living secretly among the abandoned trenches and caverns beneath the battlefield. Although passed down the generations, the rumour about the caverns was unsubstantiated. Perhaps the origin of the legend around Ghislaine lies in this same vein of battlefield visions.

Ghislaine de Féligonde is buried in the Féligonde chapel at the cemetery of Logron, the village near Chantemesle manor. The northern wall of the chapel is covered by a burgeoning bush of Ghislaine de Féligonde roses. This, however, is little in comparison to the manor's fabulous gardens. Ghislaine's father's great passion was his garden and Ghislaine's rose was planted extensively in the grounds. According to her daughter, at Chantemesle: "A magnificent specimen used to clamber up one of the north towers and that one may still be there."

The rose 'Ghislaine de Féligonde'

Type of rose: *Multiflora*
Introduced: 1916
Breeder: Turbat, Orléans, France
Parentage: *Rosa* 'Goldfinch' x *Multiflora* seedling

'Ghislaine de Féligonde' is another sumptuous rose, hardy, healthy, with ever-changing colouring. It grows to a large, tough, semi-climbing shrub, as wide as it is high, and completely covers itself with clusters of smallish double blooms. The dainty blossoms appear in a broad spectrum of shades from apricot pink to yellow to cream, so becoming of a little French countess.

Her main flowering is in the spring, with a more restrained flowering in the autumn. She is such a sight to behold in the spring that we have planted her in tough places, where she survives with aplomb and great beauty. Her habit is typical of the Multiflora family of thornless healthy ramblers, with soft green rough leaves and upright growth.

Picture Credits

The publishers should like to thank the following picture agencies, archives and individuals for their kind permission to reproduce their photographs in this book. Every care has been taken to trace copyright holders. However, if we have omitted anyone we apologise and will, if informed, add to any future edition.

Cover and p.2: Detail from "The Soul of the Rose", 1908, by John William Waterhouse (1849–1917), Private Collection. (Photo: Private Collection/By courtesy of Julian Hartnoll/ The Bridgeman Art Library)

p.10: Detail from "The Mother of the Gracchi", c.1780, by Joseph Benoit Suvée (1743–1807), Louvre, Paris. (Photo: Louvre, Paris, France/Giraudon/The Bridgeman Art Library)

pp.16–17: "The Christians Thrown to the Beasts by the Romans", 19th century, by Louis Félix Leullier (1811–82), Private Collection. (Photo: Private Collection/Photo © Bonhams, London, UK/ The Bridgeman Art Library)

p.20: Detail from "Fair Rosamund in her Bower" by William Bell Scott (1811–90), Private Collection. (Photo: Private Collection/ Photo © The Maas Gallery, London/The Bridgeman Art Library)

p.24: "The Siege of Hennebont in 1342" by the Master of the Chronicles of England and the Maitre du Froissart de Philippe de Commynes, from "Chronicles of England" by Jean de Wavrin, MS Français 76, f.61, Bibliothèque Nationale de France. (Photo: Bibliothèque Nationale de France MS Français 76, f.61)

p.28: "Yolande d'Aragon and her children kneeling before an image of the Virgin Mary and the Christ Child", from Book of Oaths and book of the foundation of the Royal Chapel of Gué de Maulny, 14th–17th century, MS 0691 f.016, Médiathèque Louis-Aragon, Le Mans. (Photo: Ville du Mans. Médiathèque Louis-Aragon/Cliché IRHT MS 0691 f.016)

p.32: Detail from "Joan of Arc", 1865 by Sir John Everett Millais (1829–96), Private Collection. (Photo: Private Collection/ Photo © Peter Nahum at The Leicester Galleries, London/ The Bridgeman Art Library)

p.38: The poet Charles d'Orléans with his wife Marie von Kleve in the castle at Blois, 1845, by Ange François (1800–1872), Musée de Brou, Bourg-en-Bresse. (Photo: akg-images/Erich Lessing)

p.43: "Amy Robsart", 1884 by William Frederick Yeames (1835–1918), Wolverhampton Art Gallery, Wolverhampton (Photo: © Wolverhampton Art Gallery, West Midlands, UK/The Bridgeman Art Library)

p.44: "Amy Robsart and Robert Dudley, Earl of Leicester", c.1827, by Richard Parkes Bonington (1802–28), Ashmolean Museum, Oxford. (Photo: Ashmolean Museum, University of Oxford, UK/ The Bridgeman Art Library)

p.48: Detail from "Miniature of Mary Queen of Scots", c.1560, by follower of François Clouet (c.1510–72), Victoria & Albert Museum, London. (Photo: Victoria & Albert Museum, London, UK/ The Bridgeman Art Library)

p.54: "Nur Jahan entertaining Jahangir and Shah Jahan", India, Mughal period, 1800, Victoria & Albert Museum, London. (Photo: © Victoria and Albert Museum, London)

p.57: "Miniature portrait of Empress Nur Jahan, wife of the Emperor Jahangir", India, Mughal period, c.1675, Victoria & Albert Museum, London. (Photo: © Victoria and Albert Museum, London)

p.60: "Portrait of Margaret Cavendish Bentinck, 2nd Duchess of Portland" by Michael Dahl (1656–1743), Private Collection. (Photo: Private Collection/Photo © Christie's Images/ The Bridgeman Art Library)

p.66–67: "The Penthièvre Family or The Cup of Chocolate", 1768, by Jean Baptiste Charpentier (1728–1806), Château de Versailles, Versailles. (Photo: Château de Versailles, France/The Bridgeman Art Library)

p.71: "Empress Joséphine at Malmaison", c.1801, by Baron François Pascal Simon Gérard (1770–1837), Musée National du Château de Malmaison, Rueil-Malmaison. (Photo: Musée National du Château de Malmaison, Rueil-Malmaison, France/Giraudon/ The Bridgeman Art Library)

p.76: Detail from "Dreams" by Edouard Frederic Wilhelm Richter (1844–1913), Galerie Nataf, Paris. (Photo: Galerie Nataf, Paris, France/ The Bridgeman Art Library)

p.82: Detail from "Madame de Sombreuil drinking a glass of blood to save the life of her father", 1853, by Pierre Puvis de Chavannes (1824–1898), Musée des Beaux-Arts, Angers (Photo: © RMN/ Michèle Bellot)

p.86: 'Madame Adélaïde d'Orléans' (oil on canvas) by Marie-Amélie Cogniet (1798–1869), Musée Condé, Chantilly. (Photo: Musée Condé, Chantilly, France/Giraudon/The Bridgeman Art Library)

p.90: Marie Thérèse Charlotte of France with her brother the Dauphin Louis-Joseph-Xavier, 1784, by Elisabeth Louise Vigée-Lebrun (1755–1842), Châteaux de Versailles et de Trianon, Versailles. (Photo: © RMN (Château de Versailles)/Gérard Blot)

p.93: "Marie-Thérèse-Charlotte Duchess of Angoulême" attributed to Friedrich Heinrich Fuger (1751–1818), Musée Condé, Chantilly. (Photo: Musée Condé, Chantilly, France/Giraudon/The Bridgeman Art Library)

p.96: "Louise Antoinette Lannes, née Guéheneuc, Duchess of Montebello and her five children", by Baron François Pascal Simon Gérard (1770–1837), Châteaux de Versailles et de Trianon, Versailles. (Photo: © RMN (Château de Versailles)/Gérard Blot)

p.99: "Portrait of the Maréchale Lannes, Duchess of Montebello" by Jean Baptiste Isabey (1767–1855), Musée du Louvre, Paris. (Photo: © RMN/Droits réservés) p.102: "Aimée Davout, Duchesse d'Auerstaedt and her two children", engraving after a painting by Henri-Pierre Danloux, from "Davout, Maréchal d'Empire, Duc d'Auerstadt, Prince d'Eckmühl, 1770–1823" by Count Henri Vigier, Paris, 1898, vol. 2., The British Library. (Photo: © The British Library Board. All Rights Reserved 010664.m.33)

p.106: Detail from "Portrait of Zoé Talon, Countess Baschi du Cayla with her two children Ugoline and Ugolin on the terrace of the Château de Saint-Ouen", 1825, by Baron François Pascal Simon Gérard (1770–1837), Châteaux de Versailles et de Trianon, Versailles. (Photo: © RMN (Château de Versailles)/El Meliani)

p.112: Detail from "Marie Louise and the King of Rome" by Baron François Pascal Simon Gérard (1770–1837), Château de Versailles, France. (Photo: Château de Versailles, France/Giraudon/The Bridgeman Art Library)

p.118–119: Detail from "Grace Darling rowing a coble in heavy seas" by Thomas Brooks, RA (1818–1891), RNLI Heritage Trust. (Photo: RNLI Heritage Trust)

p.122: "Anaïs Ségalas", by Pierre Petit (1832–1909), Archives Larousse, Paris. (Photo: Archives Larousse, Paris, France/Giraudon/ The Bridgeman Art Library)

p.126: Detail from "Queen Victoria", 1838, by Thomas Sully (1783–1872), The Wallace Collection, London. (Photo: © Wallace Collection, London, UK/The Bridgeman Art Library)

p.129: Detail from "Windsor Castle in modern time; Queen Victoria, Prince Albert and Victoria, Princess Royal", 1840–43, by Sir Edwin Landseer (1802–73). (Photo: The Royal Collection © 2011 Her Majesty Queen Elizabeth II/The Bridgeman Art Library)

p.132: "Caroline Julie Rothschild", The Rothschild Archive, London. (Photo: Reproduced with the permission of The Rothschild Archive)

p.136: "Queen Maria Hendrika" by Franz Xaver Winterhalter (1805–1873), 1863–5, Royal Collection of Belgium. (Photo: Copyright IRPA-KIK, Brussels)

p.140: "Gertrude Jekyll" by Sir William Newzam Prior Nicholson (1872–1949), 1920, National Portrait Gallery, London. (Photo: © National Portrait Gallery, London)

p.144: "Alice Marian Mills (née Harbord-Hamond), Lady Hillingdon", 18 May 1921, by Bassano, National Portrait Gallery, London. (Photo: © National Portrait Gallery, London)

p.148: "Portrait of Ellen Willmott" by Rosa Mantovani, Private Collection. (Photo: Steve Gorton)

p.152: Edith Cavell, Shoreditch Infirmary, 1903. (Photo: Getty Images)

p.156: "E.H. Wilson, Mrs. E.H. Wilson, and Muriel taken in Tokyo", 1914, Arnold Arboretum Archives, Harvard University. (Photo: © President and Fellows of Harvard College, Arnold Arboretum Archives)

p.161: "Portrait of Constance Spry" by Mollie Forestier-Walker, 1952, Private Collection. (Photo: courtesy Bonhams)

p.164: Nancy Steen, c.1966, Private Collection. (Photo: reproduced by kind permission of the daughter of Nancy Steen)

p.171: Ghislaine de Féligonde, c.1930s, Private Collection. (Photo: reproduced by kind permission of the daughter of Ghislaine de Féligonde)

Picture research by Sophie Hartley.

Acknowledgements

Author's acknowledgements
During the course of writing this book, I have drawn heavily on a wide variety of sources. Books on history, biographies, city tourist information, encyclopaedias and various websites have been used to various degrees and effect. It is not possible or even desirable to list the hundred history books and nearly seventy rose books I have consulted on the women who are featured here.

My thanks to all those scholars and all those sources of information.

For the history, I relied on the following as major references: Theo Aronson (*Napoleon and Josephine*, 1990), Napoléon Bonaparte and Empress Marie Louise (*My Dearest Louise: The Letters of Marie-Louise and Napoléon, 1813–1814*, edited by C.F. Palmstierna, 1958), Elisabeth de France (*The Life and Letters of Madame Elisabeth de France*, translated by Katharine Prescott Wormeley, 1902), Antonia Fraser (*Mary Queen of Scots*, 1969; *Marie Antoinette*, 2001), Adam Hochschild (*King Leopold's Ghost*, 1998), Richard Hough (*Victoria and Albert: Their Love and Their Tragedies*, 1996), T.E.B. Howarth (*Citizen King: The Life of Louis-Philippe*, 1961), Alan Kendall (*Robert Dudley, Earl of Leicester*, 1980), Susan McAffer (*The Charm of Nancy Steen*, 2000), Jessica Mitford (*Grace Had an English Heart*, 1988), Rebecca Stott (*The Duchess of Curiosities*, 2006), Barbara Tuchman (*A Distant Mirror*, 1978).

The Joan of Arc centre in Orléans was also an invaluable source of information.

Rose references came from the following authors: David Austin, Peter Beales, Brent Dickerson, Gerd Krüssmann, Robin Lane Fox, Hazel Le Rougetel, Bill Grant, Jack Harkness, Francois Joyeux, Phillips and Rix, Roses Anciennes en France, Stephen Scanniello, Nancy Steen, Graham Stuart Thomas, Ingrid Verdegem.

The full list of references is available at: ann.chapman@inspire.net.nz.

Photographer's acknowledgements
Paul Starosta is particularly grateful for the support of La Roseraie de Berty at Largentière, and The Roses Loubert, the Rosiers sur Loire – two producers who welcomed him to photograph the roses for this book.

Publisher's acknowledgements
The publishers would like to thank Jenny Mackewn for having introduced the project to us, Caroline Harris for editorial help, Françoise Vaslin for help with translation, and Michael Marriott and Nicola Bethell at David Austin Roses for their invaluable help with the growing notes: www.davidaustinroses.com

About the author

Ann Chapman is a passionate rose grower and an expert on Old Roses. With her husband she established the Trinity Farm Living Rose Museum in New Zealand, planting their first rose bushes over twenty-five years ago. The varieties Ann has chosen for this book come from her own gardens, where she came to wonder about the stories of the women whose namesakes she saw every day. *Women in my Rose Garden* is the result of years of research and many hours of thoughtful gardening.

About the photographer

Paul Starosta specialises in wildlife and plants, taking photographs for books and advertising campaigns all over the world. He has published more than forty books, which have been translated into several languages.

Front cover image: *The Soul of the Rose*, 1908 (oil on canvas),
John William Waterhouse (1849–1917) / Private Collection /
by courtesy of Julian Hartnoll / The Bridgeman Art Library
Back cover image: The rose 'Empress Joséphine',
photographed by Paul Starosta
Cover design: Bernard Higton